GOD'S PATTERN FOR
CREATION

GOD'S PATTERN FOR
CREATION

A COVENANTAL READING OF GENESIS 1

W. ROBERT GODFREY

P U B L I S H I N G
P.O. BOX 817 • PHILLIPSBURG • NEW JERSEY 08865-0817

Page design by Lakeside Design Plus
Typesetting by Michelle Feaster

Printed in the United States of America

Library of Congress Cataloging-in-Publication Data

Godfrey, W. Robert.
    God's pattern for creation : a covenantal reading of Genesis 1 / W. Robert Godfrey.
        p. cm.
    Includes bibliographical references.
    ISBN 0-87552-799-X (pbk.)
    1. Creationism. 2. Creationism—History of doctrines. 3. Bible. O.T. Genesis I—Criticism, interpretation, etc. I. Title.

BS651.G752 2003
222'.1106—dc22
                                                                    2003059523

To Alice and Bill Godfrey—
Loving, encouraging parents

CONTENTS

ILLUSTRATIONS

ACKNOWLEDGMENTS

I want to thank Old Testament experts who have helped me through the years. I thank Meredith G. Kline, scholar, teacher, colleague, and friend for introducing me to the joys and blessings of the Old Testament. Thanks also to Meredith M. Kline for encouraging me in many ways as fellow student and colleague. Thanks to my colleague Bryan Estelle for many hours discussing this project, reading it for me, and offering wise counsel. Any remaining errors are exclusively my responsibility.

I also thank the elders and adult Sunday school class at the Escondido United Reformed Church for letting me try out some of these ideas as I taught that class.

I thank Allan Fisher and his excellent staff at P&R for all their work in bringing this study to publication.

Finally I thank Mary Ellen, my wife, for all her encouragement as well as effective editing of this work.

Introduction

By the Word of the LORD were the heavens made, their
starry host by the breath of his mouth. Psalm 33:6

The earth is the LORD's, and everything in it, the world,
and all who live in it; for he founded it upon the seas and
established it upon the waters. Psalm 24:1–2

The Bible begins with the sweeping declaration, "In
the beginning God created the heavens and the
earth." That declaration draws us back to the beginning of time, of the universe, and of the Scriptures. It affirms the eternality and absolute sovereignty of
God. It evokes the faith and worship of God's people. It
sets the stage for all that follows in the Bible. It contrasts
biblical religion with many false teachings, among them
that there are many gods, that matter is eternal, or that the
world evolved without design or designer. Beginnings are
important, and if we want to understand the teaching of
the Bible as a whole, it is vital to understand what it
teaches about creation.

Because the doctrine of creation is so important, the interpretation of Genesis 1[1] has generated intense interest
throughout the history of the church and inspired the writing of many commentaries. In modern times the challenges

of biblical higher criticism and modern science have grown, as the early chapters of Genesis have been the focus of much of the attack on the authority and reliability of the Bible. The last twenty years have seen a great renewal of interest in this section of Scripture. Indeed the interpretation of Genesis 1 has become a matter of considerable controversy not just between conservatives and liberals but also among conservative evangelicals. Such controversy should not surprise us. Since at least the days of Augustine in the fourth century, significant differences of opinion on Genesis 1 have existed in the church among serious and faithful students of the Bible.

In some ways such controversy is a good sign for the people of God. It means that people are studying Genesis 1 with great interest and care. It also reflects the realization that several vital faith issues are linked to the meaning of the opening verses of the Bible. First, the authority of the Bible is at stake when some interpreters suggest that Genesis 1 is not true or reliable or clear in its meaning. Second, this section of the Bible helps clarify sound principles of biblical interpretation. Third, the topics presented in Genesis 1 are important for understanding the Bible as a whole and for several basic Christian doctrines. Fourth, the relationship of the Bible to modern science is a significant issue for any approach to Genesis 1.

As we study Genesis 1, we want to take a fresh look at this portion of the Bible. This is not easy to do for a passage of Scripture that is so familiar. Some people come to it with minds so settled as to its meaning that they miss important elements of its teaching. To avoid this trap we want to come to Genesis 1 eager to find all that God has to teach us. We need to pay careful attention to what God has said and how he has said it. We come trusting and confident that this is God's Word, written by Moses as part of the inerrant revelation of God. We come with the expectation that this is not a mystery but part of the history of God's people teaching them what it means to know and live for God.

A fresh look at Genesis 1 must begin by recognizing the variety of views that have existed among conservatives up to our time. Orthodox scholars have taken several different interpretive approaches to this part of the Bible in the history of the church, especially in relation to the days of creation.[2] In broad terms we can say that there are two basic views. The first and dominant view, which we will call the traditional view, sees the days of Genesis 1 as twenty-four-hour days. The other view understands the days of creation as figurative or literary expressions. This second view takes several different forms. Augustine, who taught that God had created all instantaneously, believed that the days represent God's progressive illumination of the darkness of our understanding.[3] Other interpreters have understood the days to stand for long periods of time. This view is often called the day-age interpretation. Still others see the days as providing a framework, which is not really chronological, for the relationships between elements of creation.[4] This view is often called the framework interpretation. Whatever interpretation one takes of the days of Genesis 1, most of what follows in this book should be acceptable to all those who believe that the Bible is the revelation of God. The particular interpretation of the days advocated in this study will emerge in the discussion of the text of Scripture.

The interpretation presented here draws from several different approaches and the work of many scholars. The principles of biblical analysis used here are those used by John Calvin in his commentary on Genesis 1.[5] But this interpretation is distinct from others that have come before. Developed out of a careful examination of the texts of Scripture, this study is written to communicate not primarily with scholars or ministers but with thoughtful Christian church members. It emerges from a conviction that a reliable interpretation of a significant section of the Bible must be communicable to ordinary Christians, not just specialists. This fresh look at Genesis 1 is intended as a responsible and faithful approach to the scriptural text, one that careful readers, even those not fully persuaded by this interpretation, will appreciate.

COVENANT AND THE BIBLE

The Bible teaches that all of God's relations with humankind are covenantal. The foundation for our approach to Genesis is to see that it is a part of the covenantal character of all Scripture. We cannot understand Genesis 1 until we see it covenantally.

The briefest definition of the meaning of covenant is to understand it as the divinely established relationship between humanity and God. As the Bible repeatedly states, God has said, "I will be your God, and you will be my people." These words remind us that humanity has no being or meaning apart from God. People live in fellowship with God or in rebellion against God but never independent of God. God for his part means to have a people. He created humanity for fellowship with him, and when sin destroyed that fellowship, God acted to save and preserve a people with whom that original purpose of creation would be fulfilled.

The whole Bible is covenantal because from beginning to end it shows how God is our God and how he makes us his people, first in creation and then in redemption through Christ. Although all the Bible's information is true, the Bible never provides random or abstract tidbits of knowledge. It is not an encyclopedia but a covenantal record, always focused on God and his relationship to his people.

In the Old Testament the covenant often took on a particular literary form. Such a covenant included several elements: historical background, commandments, and threats or promises. We can see that form in the Ten Commandments of Exodus 20. That summary of the covenant at Sinai between God and his people begins with historical background: "I am the LORD your God, who brought you out of Egypt, out of the land of slavery." Then the covenant has specific requirements such as "You shall not misuse the name of the LORD your God" or "Honor your father and your mother." These requirements are sometimes accompanied by specific threats to the disobedient and specific promises to the obedient. Those who misuse the name of God are warned, "for the LORD will not hold any one guiltless who misuses his name." Those who honor their parents are promised that they will "live long in the land the LORD your God is giving you."

For our purposes in studying Genesis 1 we want especially to keep in mind the importance of the element of historical background for the presentation and understanding of the covenantal relationship between God and his people. Indeed one way to see the whole Book of Genesis is as an historical introduction to God's covenant made with his people at Sinai.

GENESIS AS HISTORICAL BACKGROUND

The Book of Exodus begins by recalling how the sons of Jacob had come to Egypt and how they had multiplied there and become slaves. The book then goes on to tell how God raised up Moses to lead his people out of Egypt and how God covenanted with them at Sinai to be a nation in the midst of which God would dwell. God is interpreting for them their history as a covenant people.

The Book of Genesis provides the historical background to that covenanting at Sinai. How did Israel get to Egypt? Where had father Jacob come from, in terms of his ancestors and in terms of his homeland? The origins or roots of the people who met with God at Sinai are the central concern of the Book of Genesis.

The structure of the Book of Genesis shows that concern. Moses gave a clear structure to Genesis. It begins with an introduction (Gen. 1:1–2:3) and then has ten sections, each beginning with the words "These are the generations of . . ."[6]

Each of the ten sections is named after the father of those primarily discussed in the section (see Fig. 1).

Fig. 1. Generations in Genesis

Generations	Genesis
1. of heavens and earth	2:4–4:46
2. of Adam	5:1–6:8
3. of Noah	6:9–9:29
4. of sons of Noah	10:1–11:9
5. of Shem	11:10–26
6. of Terah	11:27–25:11
7. of Ishmael	25:12–18
8. of Isaac	25:19–35:29
9. of Esau	36:1–37:1
10. of Jacob	37:2–50:26

These generations differ greatly in length. Nearly 80 percent of Genesis (thirty-nine chapters out of fifty) deals with the time of Abraham, Isaac, Jacob, and Jacob's sons. Here is the prime focus of the book: from Abraham to Egypt.

The first five generations of the Book of Genesis (one half of the generations) are covered in ten chapters (about 20 percent of the book.) These first five generations cover a much greater period of time and contain much more important events for world history than the second five generations. But Genesis focuses particularly on the generations immediately before Egypt, because Genesis is a covenant book detailing the historical background to the

Book of Exodus. The first chapters of Genesis focus on the earlier origins of the people of God all the way back to creation and also on the emergence in history of the nations that will trouble Israel in its march to the promised land. Genesis is not a world history text, although all of its history is true. Rather it is a covenant history focusing on what the people of God need to know about their God and about themselves.

Where does Genesis 1 fit in this covenantal structure? It stands outside of the structure of the ten generations. It is the introduction to the introduction, the historical background to the historical background. If Genesis is the introduction to Exodus, Genesis 1 is the introduction to Genesis, detailing the grand story of creation and the meaning of creation before the entrance of sin into the world. It is the only section in the Bible in which sin is not a present reality. Even the first generation (Gen. 2:4–4:46) is marred by the fall of the world into sin. This introduction is also a part of covenant history, history for us as the people of God who need to know their origins and God's design for them.

1

THE FIRST THREE DAYS OF CREATION

Genesis 1:1–13

With this brief overview of the Book of Genesis and its purpose in covenant history, we are ready to look at the text of Genesis 1. We want to try to follow the mind of Moses as he lays out the revelation of God's creative work. We want in particular to approach its understanding as an ancient Israelite would. This text is not a secret revelation of modern science or an invitation to flights of philosophical speculation. Genesis 1 is a straightforward account of creation and its meaning. But we must also remember that the faithful Israelite did not believe that he learned the revelation of God by just glancing at the text. Genesis 1 is the beginning of the Torah or Law, and the psalmist tells us of the blessed man, "his delight is in the law of the LORD, and on his law he meditates day and night" (Ps. 1:2). To understand God's Word we must meditate on it, return to it again and again, and roll it around in our minds. Like the ancient believers, we must enjoy the work of searching the Scriptures and enjoying their riches and depths.

THE BEGINNING

In the beginning God created the heavens and the earth. (Gen. 1:1)

The opening words of Genesis 1 are among the grandest in the Bible: "In the beginning God created the heavens and the earth." Here is the declaration of God's absolute control of creation. This verse expresses the critical biblical truth that God existed before and independent of creation. Even before the beginning of time and the universe, there was God. His existence is the foundation of all that is created. He made all of creation out of nothing. All things in the heavens and on earth are the result of God's creative acts. They exist at his will and do not have any power over against him.

The God who created in Genesis 1:1 is not introduced or explained in this text. The assumption is that the people of Israel knew their God and who he was. This again reminds us that Genesis is not written as a history book for uninformed, worldwide readers but is part of the covenant history written for a covenant people who already know their God.

The God revealed in the Bible is radically different from the ancient gods of the Near East. Those gods did not create matter but only shaped it. The struggle between the gods and the chaotic matter was at the heart of many ancient pagan creation tales. The God of the Bible by contrast sovereignly creates matter and without struggle or difficulty shapes it according to his will.

The word translated "created" in Genesis 1:1 is used only of the work of God in the Old Testament. That usage points to the unique character of the work of God in creation. Only he could have done it. Only he did it. That word can also be translated "made." God in the creation is the great maker. Unlike humans, however, God makes the materials he uses out of nothing as well as shapes them to his purpose.

The revelation of God as the all-powerful creator is not just information for the world. It is a message to the covenant people about the character of their God. Notice the use of this truth, for example, in Psalm 124. There the psalmist reflects on the dangers of his life and the many enemies that surround and threaten him. As he praises God for delivering his people, he concludes the psalm with the words, "Our help is in the name of the LORD, the Maker of heaven and earth." His point is that however great our enemies are, our God is greater because he created the entire universe that surrounds us. Nothing is too great for him to do. And he is the help of his people in the face of every enemy.

The revelation of God as creator then is a key part of our faith for living the Christian life as God's covenant people. And only faith really grasps this truth. As Hebrews 11:3 reminds us, "By faith we understand that the universe was formed at God's command, so that what is seen was not made out of what was visible." The biblical doctrine of creation can be grasped only by faith and is an article of our faith.

NOW THE EARTH

Now the earth was formless and empty, darkness was over the surface of the deep, and the Spirit of God was hovering over the waters. (Gen. 1:2)

After declaring that God created the heavens and the earth, Genesis 1:2 turns the focus of its attention not to the heavens or the whole universe but to the earth: "Now the earth was formless and empty, darkness was over the surface of the deep, and the Spirit of God was hovering over the waters." This text is often rather neglected by interpreters, but in fact it is important to the story of creation. The point of this text is not, as some have suggested, that the world was a chaos and that God, like the ancient pagan gods, had to battle the chaos to form it. The image of the Spirit of God hovering like a great bird[1] over the waters is an image of God's quiet and complete control over his creation.

This text still may surprise us. Why did God leave himself with more to do on the earth? Why not complete the work all at once or at least not dwell on the deficiencies of the earth in Genesis 1:2? Two important points emerge. First, God shows us that his purpose in creation is not some kind of static, unchanging reality. Just as time is built into creation from the beginning, so is development. God in his creation is already pointing us to a fulfillment or consummation of that creation. Theologians would say that God builds eschatology into creation at the beginning. God is already preparing us for the idea of a final completion of his work that is more developed than what is created at first. The end will be better than the beginning. Even apart from sin, the new heaven and the new earth will be more glorious than the first heaven and the first earth.

Second, Genesis 1:2 shows us that God's creative purpose is not for himself but rather culminates in the creation of humanity. A world that is empty or covered with water or dark is not a problem for God's existence. The point of Genesis 1:2 is that the earth God had brought into being was not yet a habitable place for the creature with whom God would have a covenantal relationship. God will act to form and arrange the world as a proper dwelling place for his image bearers. Genesis 1:2 is critical for understanding the rest of the creation narrative because the three elements that rendered the earth uninhabitable for humanity are dealt with one at a time in God's subsequent acts of creation. These problems are a key to understanding what God is revealing about the meaning of creation in Genesis 1.

God, then, faces three obstacles to people living on the earth. First, the world was formless and empty. (The terms used here are used elsewhere in the Bible to describe an uninhabitable desert.[2] The sense is not a formless chaos but rather a barren waste.) Second, the earth was dark. Third, waters covered the earth. These elements, again, do not mean the world was chaos or resisted God in any way. Rather they are the building blocks that God had created and would use to construct a world for man.

THE FIRST DAY

And God said, "Let there be light," and there was light. God saw that the light was good, and he separated the light from the darkness. God called the light "day," and the darkness he called "night." And there was evening, and there was morning—the first day. (Gen. 1:3–5)

As we come to the days of creation beginning in Genesis 1:3, it is important to remember that Moses presents the creation of the heavens and the earth in Genesis 1:1–2 without reference to days. Moses gives no indication of time elapsed, if any, between Genesis 1:2 and Genesis 1:3. Time is not his focus or concern. Day one is not presented as the beginning of creation but as the shaping and filling of creation for humankind according to God's purposes.

The first problem posed in Genesis 1:2 that God addresses is the problem of darkness. Light and dark are the same to God in the sense that he needs neither for the glory of his existence. Nor does he need light in order to see. As the psalmist declares of God, "Even the darkness will not be dark to you; the night will shine like day, for darkness is as light to you" (Ps. 139:12). Rather light is necessary for human existence and is so foundational that it becomes a symbol and synonym for human life. Psalm 18:28 says, "You, O Lord, keep my lamp burning; my God turns my darkness into light." And Psalm 112:4 says, "Even in darkness light dawns for the upright, for the gracious and compassionate and righteous man."

In response to the problem of darkness, we read the words, "And God said . . ." We should not rush past these words assuming that we know what they must mean. Rather we should pause to ponder them. They are familiar because often in the Bible God speaks directly to people, and the whole Bible is his Word. But what is God revealing to us here? In the context of Genesis 1:3 no human existed to hear him. Is God telling us that he has a mouth and vocal cords? Even if we speculate that he is speaking to the angels, are we to assume that they have ears? God and the angels are spirit beings. God represents himself as speaking, not to describe who he is in himself or even to describe precisely what he did but to communicate to us human beings what he did in words that we can understand. Genesis 1:3 is parallel to Psalm 33:6, "By the word of the LORD were the heavens made, their starry host by the breath of his mouth." The point of both texts is not to make God into a physical being. He does not have a mouth or vocal cords, any more than describing God's Spirit as hovering means that God is a bird. Rather the Bible is emphasizing the ease of creation for God. Words and breath are the most effortless actions of men. But our words are often a waste of breath. They often do not accomplish what we wish. But for our God, his power is so great that his barest wishes come into being.

Perhaps God's revelation of himself as speaking at the beginning of creation is also a preparation for the truth that

God the Father created in the beginning through the Word, his eternal Son. John 1:1–5 is clearly a reflection on and an expansion of the Genesis story of creation. John takes us back to the beginning and declares that the Word was there and was God. Then he writes of the Word: "Through him all things were made; without him nothing was made that has been made" (John 1:3).

The God who speaks with such power speaks to solve the problem of darkness. God creates light. Our amazement at the wonder and power of God's word to create light, which is so fundamental to our life and experience, may lead us to stop at this point and say simply that on the first day God created light. But God did more than create light. Indeed had he only created light, we would not have had a first day. What God did was first to create light and then to separate light from darkness. Throughout the story of creation not only does God bring something—in this case light—into existence, but also he orders it and gives it a function. By separating and ordering light and darkness, he gives to both of them a purpose, namely, to be day and night, to be the orderly succession of evening and morning. What God ultimately created on the first day was day. Light was the prelude to creating the day.

Notice that the first use of the word *day* (Hebrew *yom*) in Genesis 1 is to refer to daylight (Gen. 1:5). Day is contrasted to night. Those who insist that "day" in Genesis 1 is obviously a reference to twenty-four-hour days should pause to remember that the first use of day in the text does not have that meaning.

The first great creative act of God, then, is not simply creating light. Rather he creates day for humankind. God's activity on the first day is to create light so that man will have a day. It is as much about ordering time as it is about light. In order to live and work, to fulfill the purpose of God for his image bearer, man needs not just light. He needs day and night. God creates and orders not just as a display of his power but to show us the meaning of his creation and humanity's place in it. Psalm 104:20–23 reflects on this aspect of creation, noting that the day is the time for man to go forth to work: "You bring darkness, it becomes night, and all the beasts of the forest prowl. The lions roar for their prey and seek their food from God. The sun rises, and they steal away; they return and lie down in their dens. Then man goes out to his work, to his labor until evening." Daylight is the realm of man's labor.

The Bible explicitly describes the creation of day and night as part of the fixed and certain world that God has made for man, his covenant creature. Indeed the Bible refers to this act of creation as a covenant: "This is what the LORD says: 'If you can break my covenant with the day and my covenant with the night, so that day and night no longer come at their appointed time, then my covenant with David my servant . . . can be broken.' . . . This is what the LORD says: 'If I have not established my covenant with day and night and the fixed laws of heaven and earth, then I will reject the descendants of Jacob' " (Jer. 33:20–26). God made the same point about the certainty of days after the flood when he promised, "As long as the earth endures, seedtime and harvest, cold and heat, summer and winter, day and night will never cease" (Gen. 8:22). God's covenant promises are as certain as the covenantal succession of day and night.

The first day of creation continues with the statement that God saw that the light was good. Here again we can see that the text is a revelation for us, his creatures. God did not need to analyze and evaluate his work to decide that it was good. He knew immediately that it was good and that because of his character it could not be anything other than good. Our good God can only do good. The recording of the goodness of creation is a revelation to us so that we might know the goodness of the work of God. Against those who might think that matter is evil and opposed to spirit or that God battles the chaos to bring order, stand the simple but profound words that God made all the created order, made it easily, and made it good.

The creation of light and day ends with words that will almost become a refrain in the rest of Genesis 1: "And there was evening, and there was morning—the first day." Here for the first time the word *day* is used to refer to the period including light and darkness. (Perhaps Genesis sees the day as evening and morning because the darkness was first and then the light.) But we should note that we cannot assume that this is a twenty-four-hour day, because the sun, which is appointed to mark days for us (Gen. 1:14), does not appear until the fourth day. We will wait until our consideration of the fourth day to discuss the source of the light that God created on the first day and how that bears on our interpretation of the meaning of the days.

THE SECOND DAY

And God said, "Let there be an expanse between the waters to separate water from water." So God made the expanse and separated the water under the expanse from the water above it. And it was so. God called the expanse "sky." And there was evening, and there was morning—the second day. (Gen. 1:6–8)

On the second day God begins to address the second problem of Genesis 1:2—the problem of the waters that cover the earth. If there is to be a place for humans, the waters too must be separated and ordered. The first act of separating the waters is the creation of an expanse or firmament that separates the waters into upper and lower waters. Here we see Moses giving a description of God's creative act from the perspective of what the common man sees and experiences in this world. Genesis 1:6–8 is not a detailed scientific description of reality but a presentation of what we see. We see that there are lower waters on the earth and upper waters that produce rain. We also see that between those waters is a space that Moses called the firmament or expanse that we would call the sky. That separation of waters and that expanse is what God brought into being on the second day.

By describing the creation on day two in terms of human perspective, God reminds us again that Genesis 1 is for us. The character of the revelation is not to tell us about creation in the abstract but about the appearance and meaning of creation for God's image bearer. Genesis 1 is not an encyclopedia of history or science but a covenant

31

revelation of the character of the creation that God made for man.

God's work on the second day closes with the familiar words, "And there was evening, and there was morning—the second day." Those words are so familiar we may miss the point: Moses is reminding us that the work of the first day carries over to the second day. On the second day we have not only the new work of separating the waters but also the continuation of the work of the first day, namely, the creation of the day.

Many interpreters have observed that God does not declare his acts on the second day as good. Why is that? The first reason is that God had not completed his work on the waters. By withholding his word of evaluation God points to the fact that the work on the waters is not completed until the third day. Only then does he call it good. In that way he shows the close link in meaning between the second and third day.

The second reason is that God wants to indicate that the days of creation are not the only structure of Genesis 1. Since days two and three together solve one of the problems of Genesis 1:2, God reminds us that more is happening in the text than simply recording the days.

In fact the absence of the words "and God saw that it was good" should give us pause to reflect on the subtle structural elements that Moses has worked into the text. We are told seven times in Genesis 1 that God saw the goodness of his work. But those seven statements do not correspond to the seven days. Rather no statement about the goodness of creation is made on days two and seven.

Two declarations of the goodness of creation are made on days three and six. So we see seven as an important element of the text quite apart from the seven days. (We can also note that the phrase "and it was so" is repeated seven times.) But seven is not the only important number in the text. Ten times we are told that "God said," and of those ten, seven are before the creation of man and three are in relation to the creation of man. We also find that the phrase "let there be" and the word *make* are used ten times. Also the word *create* is used in three verses: Genesis 1:1, 1:21, and 1:27. In Genesis 1:27 it is used three times.[3] So Moses' complex use of seven, ten, and three points to the careful literary structure given to this portion of Scripture. This careful composition shows that Moses has reflected deeply on every word he has used and wants us to see that the text is constructed not only around seven days but around many other elements as well.

THE THIRD DAY

And God said, "Let the water under the sky be gathered to one place, and let dry ground appear." And it was so. God called the dry ground "land," and the gathered waters he called "seas." And God saw that it was good.

Then God said, "Let the land produce vegetation: seed-bearing plants and trees on the land that bear fruit with seed in it, according to their various kinds." And it was so. The land produced vegetation: plants bearing seed according to their kinds and trees bearing fruit with seed in it according to their kinds. And

God saw that it was good. And there was evening, and there was morning—the third day. (Gen. 1:9–13)

On the third day God continues the work of dealing with the problem of making the earth habitable for humanity. He returns to dealing with the problem of water. Man must have for his existence not only water, rain, and sky; he must also have land. So God separates the waters from the land and sets boundaries for the seas that they cannot cross. Ancient pagans saw the waters of the seas as great threats to the world, but the Scriptures frequently celebrate how easily God controls the seas. They are no problem or threat for him: "He set the earth on its foundations; it can never be moved. You covered it with the deep as with a garment; the waters stood above the mountains. But at your rebuke the waters fled, at the sound of your thunder they took to flight; they flowed over the mountains, they went down into the valleys, to the place you assigned for them. You set a boundary they cannot cross; never again will they cover the earth" (Ps. 104:5–9). The same point is also made in Job 38:8–11: "Who shut up the sea behind doors when it burst forth from the womb, when I made the clouds its garment and wrapped it in thick darkness, when I fixed limits for it and set its doors and bars in place, when I said, 'This far you may come and no farther; here is where your proud waves halt.' " Wisdom also testifies: "I was there when he set the heavens in place, when he marked out the horizon on the face of the deep, when he established the clouds above and fixed securely the fountains of the deep, when he gave the sea its boundary so the waters would not overstep his command, and when he marked out the foundations of the earth. Then I was the craftsman at his side. I was filled with delight day after day, rejoicing always in his presence" (Prov. 8:27–30). On the third day God finishes solving the problem of the waters and declares his work good.

God has not, however, finished the work of the third day. He continues by creating the vegetation on the dry land. He distinguishes types of vegetation: plants and trees. The creation of this vegetation is mentioned with humanity in mind, since the vegetation is specifically appointed as food for man in the sixth day (Gen. 1:29).

A distinctive aspect of the creation of vegetation is that God commands the earth to sprout and bring forth the vegetation. Rather than creating the vegetation directly, God creates it through the means of the earth. The vegetation grew out of the ground rather than appearing on it. We must remember that God acts just as truly and effectively when he works through means as when he works directly.

The third day is parallel to the sixth in its two quite distinct acts of creation and its two declarations of the goodness of the acts of the day. These similarities remind us of the intricate structure and interrelationships of the text.

The third day again not only records the creative acts of that day but also alludes to the creative events of the earlier days. The waters separated, the sky, and the day are also mentioned along with the dry land and the vegetation.

2

THE FINAL FOUR DAYS OF CREATION

Genesis 1:14–2:3

The third problem Genesis 1:2 presents is the problem of a world that is empty. God begins by filling the sky with lights as he will later fill the sea with fish, the sky with birds, and the land with animals and people.

THE FOURTH DAY

And God said, "Let there be lights in the expanse of the sky to separate the day from the night, and let them serve as signs to mark seasons and days and years, and let them be lights in the expanse of the sky to give light on the earth." And it was so. God made two great lights—the greater light to govern the day and the lesser light to govern the night. He also made the stars. God set them in the expanse of the sky to give light on the earth, to govern the day and the night, and to separate light from darkness. And God saw that it was good. And there was evening, and there was morning—the fourth day. (Gen. 1:14–19)

We come now to the fourth day, which is one of the key days in terms of the structure and interpretation of Genesis 1. First, we can see that the fourth day continues the pattern of responding to the problems with the earth described in Genesis 1:2. God solves the problem of darkness in one day. He solves the problem of water covering the earth in two days (days two and three). Then he solves the problem of an empty world in three days (days four, five, and six). This progression of days is a way of emphasizing the importance of what is done to fill the earth since God gives more time to it. This pattern is another pointer to the focus of the text on the creation of a habitable world for man in which he can have fellowship with God.

Second, we can see that God assigns specific functions to the lights that he creates. They are to give light to the earth, to separate the day from the night, and to govern day and night. Part of that governing or ruling includes serving as signs to mark the seasons, days, and years. The text underscores the importance of these functions by the length of the description of these functions (longer than any day so far) and by significant repetition of those functions (also different from any day so far). This feature of the text reinforces its importance in Genesis 1. Notice the fourfold presentation of the lights and their functions (see Fig. 2).

Fig. 2. Lights in Genesis 1:14–17

The Lights in Genesis 1:14–17

Verse	Function
14	To separate To be signs
15	To give light on the earth
16	To govern
17	To give light on the earth To govern To separate

Notice more particularly the relationship of these functions in the shape of the text in Figure 3.

Fig. 3. Chiasm in Genesis 1:14–17

```
A     to separate (v. 14a)
  B     to be signs (v. 14b)
    C     to give light on the earth (v. 15)
      D     to govern (v. 16)
    C'    to give light on the earth (v. 17a)
  D'    to govern (v. 17b)
A'    to separate (v. 17c)
```

One commentator calls this arrangement of the text "a well-organized concentric structure."[1] More technically, scholars call this structure a chiasm. Nils Lund defined this literary form in these words: "According to its Greek origin the term designates a literary figure, or principle, which consists of 'a placing crosswise' of words in a sentence. The term is used in rhetoric to designate an inversion of the order of words or phrases which are repeated or subsequently referred to in the sentence."[2] Lund states that this structure is very common in Old Testament Hebrew and offers several examples. One simple example is Psalm 51:2, "Thoroughly wash me from my iniquity, and from my sin cleanse me."[3] The chiasm is clear when we diagram it as in Figure 4.

Fig. 4. Chiasm in Psalm 51:2

    A   Thoroughly wash me
      B   from my iniquity
      B'   and from my sin
    A'   cleanse me.

Such a diagram helps us to see the relationship between the various elements of the text and helps make clear that sin and iniquity on the one hand and wash and cleanse on the other hand refer to the same things.

Returning to the fourth day and the functions of the lights, the chiastic structure shows again the intricacy with which Moses put this text together. The irregularity of this chiasm (compare B and D) suggests that the function of the lights as signs (B) is another way of expressing governing (D). Governing then is at the heart of the function of the lights as they rule over the day, the night, and the seasons.

Seeing this chiasm at the heart of the fourth day encourages us to consider the structural relationships between this day and other parts of Genesis 1. Notice the several points of correspondence that exist between the first and the fourth days of creation. On the first day God created the light, and on the fourth day God created the lights to give light. On the first day God separated the light from the darkness. On the fourth day the lights are appointed to separate the day from the night. On the first day the source of light is the word and will of God, while on the fourth day the source of light is the lights (sun, moon, and stars) that God makes. Exactly the same relationship to light is ascribed to the word and will of God on day one and to the lights on day four. The lights give light to the earth (Gen. 1:15, 17). The closeness of the relationship is underscored by the identity of words used on the two days and especially by the reiteration of the function of the lights (Gen. 1:14–18).

How do we account for these similarities between the first and fourth days? One option, the traditional interpretation, suggests that God changes the relationship between light and the source of light from day one to day four. The traditional interpretation argues that on days one, two, and three there was some other created source for the light than the lights of the fourth day. (The source must be a created source since God has called into being that which had not existed before. That is to say that the light did not shine from the being of God.) The idea of a different source for light on the first three days is certainly possible since our God can do whatever pleases him. Many in the history of the church, including John Calvin and Francis Turretin, have argued that position.

The traditional interpretation, however, does not give adequate attention to the way in which the days of creation are addressing the problems of Genesis 1:2. The creation of the lights on day four is addressing not the problem of darkness but the problem of the emptiness of the sky. The text seems to suggest that day four is not about the creation of a new and different source for the light created on day one but rather is now pointing us to the lights that fill the sky and that always were the source of light. In other words, day one and day four describe the same creative act of God from different perspectives and as solutions to different problems posed in Genesis 1:2.

Are there other lines of evidence that support the conclusion that day one and day four describe the same act of God to serve different purposes in the text? There are two. First, we should note that such a conclusion is consonant with what we know about the ways in which God works through means. We know that God works as truly and effectively when he works through means as when he works immediately. We see that in Psalm 104:19–20: "The moon marks off the seasons, and the sun knows when to go down. You bring darkness, it becomes night." This psalm attributes the coming of darkness to God and to the sun going down. But there are not two sources of the coming darkness. The one source is God working through the movements of the sun. The idea of God working through a means was introduced in Genesis 1, on day three, when God commanded the earth to sprout vegetation. So the idea that God creates light and uses a means for light are not necessarily contradictory or unbiblical. We find the same is true with the creation of man on the sixth day. In Genesis 1 it seems that God created man immediately and simply by the word of his power. But Genesis 2:7 tells us that God formed man by using the means of the dust of the earth. The creation of man is a case parallel to the creation of light, where the creation is described first and only later is the means God used introduced.

Second, we should notice that elsewhere the Bible always links the light to the lights. The Bible seems to say that in this world the light comes from the lights until the day of the new heaven and the new earth: "The city does not need the sun or the moon to shine on it, for the glory of God gives it light, and the Lamb is its lamp" (Rev. 21:23). "There will be no more night. They will not need the light of a lamp or the light of the sun, for the Lord God will give them light" (Rev. 22:5). This vision of John's is a fulfillment of Isaiah 60:19–20: "The sun will no more be your light by day, nor will the brightness of the moon shine on you, for the LORD will be your everlasting light, and your God will be your glory. Your sun will never set again, and your moon will wane no more; the LORD will be your everlasting light, and your days of sorrow will end." It also fulfills Zechariah 14:6–7: "On that day there will be no light, no cold or frost. It will be a unique day, without daytime or nighttime—a day known to the LORD. When evening comes, there will be light." These statements of Scripture all describe the great day of glory and renewal for the people of God in the new heaven and the new earth. The glory and presence of God will be such that the sun and moon will no longer be needed as the source of light. Such statements surely imply that in the old heaven and earth light came only from the lights. Notice in particular how Zechariah stresses that this new situation is unique, unlike anything that daytime has known before. That reference to daytime takes us back to day one of Genesis 1, when that daytime was created.

Psalm 74:16–17 makes the same point about the light and lights with reference to creation: "The day is yours, and yours also the night; you established the sun and moon. It was you who set all the boundaries of the earth; you made both summer and winter." Here God is described as setting the boundary between day and night in relation to the sun and moon. God created the day, and he created the sun. The psalmist assumes that the sun rules the day and that God's creation of the day is through the sun. God's use of the sun in this text in no way diminishes the truth that God created the day. The psalmist's way of relating the day to the sun is the same as the way in which we see days one and four in Genesis 1 as describing the same act of creation.

If we conclude that days one and four seem to describe the same activity of God from different perspectives, then we must conclude that the days of creation in Genesis 1 are not simple chronology. If the days are not straightforward chronology, what are they? We will not see the full answer to that question until we get to day seven. But here we should pause to observe that throughout the Bible texts are arranged in ways that appear to be simple chronology when they are something else.

The first category of biblical texts in which such an arrangement occurs is in accounts that seem to be organized chronologically but are organized topically. A clear example of this category is present in the temptations of Christ recorded in the Gospels of Matthew and Luke. Each account seems to describe a straightforward story of the devil coming to tempt Jesus three times, each confrontation following chronologically on the other. But since the same order is not given in each Gospel, the confrontations are obviously not chronological in one or both of the Gospels.

An author in the Bible often arranges his historical material in topical ways to make some particular point. A good example can be found in the history of King Joash recorded in 2 Kings 13–14.[4] There we read a brief comment on Joash, and in 2 Kings 13:13 we are told that he died. We naturally think we are done with Joash. But the text goes on to write of Joash and then record his death in 2 Kings 14:16. Was Joash resurrected between the first and second record of his reign? No. Clearly the material is arranged topically: first his domestic policy and then his foreign policy. The principle of arrangement, apparently chronological, was in fact topical. This part of biblical history is just as much reliable history in a topical form as it is in a chronological form.

Commentators such as John Calvin have noticed this phenomenon of topical arrangement especially in the writings of Moses. Calvin wrote, "There is no reason why any one should be surprised that the order of the narrative is changed, since it plainly appears from many passages that the order of time is not always observed by Moses."[5] He added, "We know that it was a figure of speech in common use with the Hebrews to touch upon the chief points of a matter and then to fill up, in the progress of the history, what had been omitted."[6] While Calvin does not apply this principle to Genesis 1, we are following his methods of interpretation in reaching such a conclusion.

Another category of such biblical texts is accounts in which numbered chronological periods seem to be the point of the text but some other message is communicated. A familiar example is the reference to one thousand years in Revelation 20. Many evangelicals have declared, "The meaning of that text is obvious. It means simply a thousand years. The Bible means what it says. If we take an approach to interpretation that sees the thousand years as symbolic of something else, we undermine the literal meaning of the text and are on a slippery slope toward denying many of the teachings of the Bible." But most Reformed interpreters of the Book of the Revelation have rejected such an interpretation of Revelation 20. They have argued that Revelation is full of symbols, especially symbolic uses of the numbers three, seven, ten, twelve, and multiples of those numbers. John signals such symbolic uses of numbers in the first chapter: "John, to the seven churches in the province of Asia: Grace and peace to you from who him is, and who was, and who is to come, and from the seven spirits before his throne, and from Jesus Christ, who is the faithful witness, the firstborn from the dead, and the ruler of the kings of the earth" (Rev. 1:4–5).

John's blessing is certainly trinitarian, but the Father is presented in the threefold character of him who was and is and is to come. The Son is also presented in a threefold description as witness, firstborn, and ruler. The Holy Spirit is presented as seven spirits before the throne. Does this literally mean that there are nine persons in the Godhead? Of course not! Seven is the number of completion and fullness. Most likely John writes of seven spirits here to indicate that each of the seven churches has the Holy Spirit.[7] Since these symbolic numbers appear throughout the book, Reformed interpreters tend to see the thousand years as a symbol of the whole history of the church from the first to the second coming of Christ. Such interpreters insist that they are presenting the literal meaning of the text according to good principles of exegesis.[8]

Of this category of texts perhaps the closest parallel in Scripture to Genesis 1 is the apparent chronology of Matthew's genealogy of Jesus. The parallel is close in three ways. First, the word *generation* is as clearly chronological as is the word *day*. Second, the generations in Matthew are divided into three groups of fourteen generations each. So the chronological term *generation* is modified by the specific number fourteen. Third, Matthew's genealogy is linked to the Book of Genesis by the words of Matthew 1:1, "the book of the generations" KJV (*biblos geneseōs*). Those are the same words used in the Greek Septuagint version of the Old Testament to introduce the generations of Genesis 2:4, 5:1, and so on.

What did Matthew mean when he wrote, "Thus there were fourteen generations in all from Abraham to David, fourteen from David to the exile to Babylon, and fourteen from the exile to the Christ" (Matt. 1:17)? The answer seems clear and straightforward, namely, that fourteen chronological generations occurred between each of the events that he highlighted. But we know from Matthew and from other parts of the Bible that that simple reading of the text is wrong. Matthew gives a clear indication that no simple chronology is intended when in his third group of fourteen generations he lists only thirteen generations. By comparing Matthew with other scriptural accounts of the generations, we also see that Matthew is not giving a simple chronology. For example, Luke lists twenty generations between David and the exile and twenty-two generations from the exile to Jesus.

We should not be surprised to discover that genealogies in the Bible omit generations. For example, Luke lists twelve generations from Adam to Abraham, but Genesis lists twenty generations for that same period. What is surprising is that Matthew seems to make such a strong chronological point about the fourteen generations when his point cannot have been primarily chronological. Strict chronological sequence is subordinated to theological concerns. Commentators have suggested various explanations as to what he did mean,[9] but all recognize that what was apparently chronological had another meaning, as Scripture shows. The same, then, could be true of Genesis 1.

Why would Genesis 1 have an apparently chronological form? One partial answer is that a succession of days is presented in the text because each day of creation carries with it references to the creative accomplishments of the earlier days. Therefore each act of creation contains a reference to day because "day" was the first creative act. We can see this reiteration in the fourth day in reference to the elements created on earlier days: the day, the light, the sky, the earth (presumably including the seas and the dry land), and the vegetation (implied in seasons governed by the sun and moon). And when God saw that it was good, he was viewing not only the lights that he had created but also the accumulated works of all his previous activities.

The full answer to the chronological form of Genesis 1 must wait until we get to the seventh day. There we can consider fully the way in which the days of creation make up a week and the true meaning of that week of days. Here, however, we can further note the chiastic structure connecting the first, fourth, and seventh days of Genesis 1. The lights created on the fourth day do not only give light and separate the day from the night. We are also told that they—the sun and the moon—govern or rule the day and the night. That ruling not only involves the giving of light but also involves serving "as signs to mark seasons and days and years." The signs of these lights signal the divisions of time and also seasons of the year, perhaps both growing seasons and the seasons of holy days for Israel. God makes the lights to rule and govern the day and the night. The lights of the fourth day give the light of the first day. The lights that govern the days and seasons mark the seventh day, the Sabbath of the people of God, to teach Israel to rest. So we see how closely the first, fourth, and seventh days of the creation are tied together. We can represent this chiasm as in Figure 5.[10]

Fig. 5. Chiasm First, Fourth, and Seventh Days

A   creation of the day (governed by the lights)
   B   creation of separated waters, sky, land, and vegetation
      C   creation of the lights to govern the day and seasons
   B'   creation of fish, birds, land animals and man
A'   appointment of day of rest (marked as a recurring season by the lights)

We can express this chiasm as A, B, C, B´, A´. The first and last elements are related, as are the second and fourth. The middle element has a central, organizing function. A is the work of creating the day and A´ is the appointment of the day of rest. C is the day on which the ruler of the days and seasons is created.

The presence of a chiasm tying the days of creation together shows us again how carefully constructed the story of creation is and reminds us to think seriously about what Moses is telling us. Here as elsewhere in Scripture the meaning is found in the form as well as the words of the text.

THE FIFTH DAY

And God said, "Let the water teem with living creatures, and let birds fly above the earth across the expanse of the sky." So God created the great creatures of the sea and every living and moving thing with which the water teems, according to their kinds, and every winged bird according to its kind. And God saw that it was good. God blessed them and said, "Be fruitful and increase in number and fill the water in the seas, and let the birds increase on the earth."And there was evening, and there was morning— the fifth day. (Gen. 1:20–23)

On the fifth day God continues to fill the earth as part of his solution to the problem of an empty world. He begins to fill the waters with fish and the skies with birds. He also blessed the fish and the birds that they would be fruitful, the fish to fill the seas and the birds to increase on the earth. (The birds are related to the sky, where they fly, and to the earth, where they nest.)

On this fifth day the reiteration of the earlier aspects of creation are again mentioned or alluded to: the day (and implicitly the sun), the water, and the land (and implicitly the vegetation).

Now that we have looked at the first five days, we have reached a good point at which to pause and consider aspects of one approach to interpreting Genesis 1 often called the framework interpretation. This view treats the days of Genesis 1 as a figurative framework for revealing God's work of creation. A recent essay defending this interpretation grounds it on three key points.[11] The first point the authors call "the two Triads." This point stresses the division of the six days of creation into two sections, usually called the kingdoms of the first three days and the kings of the second three days. We can see these two triads clearly in Figure 6.

Fig. 6. Two Triads in Genesis 1

Kingdoms	Kings
Day 1: day and night	Day 4: sun, moon, and stars
Day 2: division of waters and sky	Day 5: fish and birds
Day 3: seas, land, and vegetation	Day 6: animals and man

This recognition of the two triads is useful: the lights do rule the day and night, birds may rule the sky, fish may rule the waters, animals may rule the land, and man is king of all these kings.

Nevertheless this insight has limits. First, by itself the recognition of two triads does not show that the days are figurative. Second, Genesis 1 does not explicitly describe the birds as ruling the sky or the fish as ruling the sea. Third, days two and five do not correspond as one would expect in a strict listing of kingdoms and kings. For days two and five to follow the division of kingdoms and kings strictly, the fish should have been created on day six. The lack of exact correspondence at this point is not a major problem, however, since Hebrew literary structure often artfully varies forms so that they are not exactly balanced.

The second point made in this essay on the framework view refers to Genesis 2:5. There we read that there was no vegetation on the earth because it had not rained. The framework interpretation argues that if vegetation grows by the ordinary means of rain, then the ordinary providence that guides the growth of plants is at work on the third day of creation. But would the land produce vegetation (Gen. 1:11) by ordinary means in just twenty-four hours on the third day? Does not Genesis 2:5 rather lead us to conclude that the third day is not a twenty-four hour day but a literary figure? And if ordinary providence is at work in day three, then is it not likely that the same ordinary providence should guide us to see the light of day one and the lights of day four as describing the same creative event?

This point is the strongest made for the framework view. Its critics, however, argue that since creation involves a variety of miraculous acts on the part of God, we cannot with certainty know when God has acted miraculously and when he acts according to ordinary providence. Still Genesis 2:5 does seem clearly to relate the growth of vegetation to the ordinary providence of rain.

The third point for the framework view is called "the two-register cosmology." Here the argument is that Genesis 1:1 describes the creation of two realms: the heavens, a spiritual reality where God and his angels dwell, and the earth, which is the visible world, including the sky. The days of Genesis 1 are seen as part of the heavenly realm of God and are therefore not earthly twenty-four-hour days. The defenders of this idea point especially to the seventh day, maintaining that since that day is God's day of rest without an evening and morning, it must be an eternal day. Therefore if day seven is not a twenty-four-hour day, neither are the others.

A response to this point would require a full discussion of the seventh day, to which we will turn at the appropriate time. Here we will simply note that while the "two-register cosmology" is present in Scripture, it is not clear that it is a helpful key with reference to the days of Genesis 1. Genesis 1:2 focuses our attention on the earth, not on the heavenly realm. From that focus follow the days of Genesis 1, which are all about the creation of the visible world, including the creation of day itself. Further, the framework's approach to the days of Genesis 1 as figurative does not seem fully to explain the chronological and sequential character of the text.

THE SIXTH DAY

And God said, "Let the land produce living creatures according to their kinds: livestock, creatures that move along the ground, and wild animals, each according to its kind." And it was so. God made the wild animals according to their kinds, the livestock according to their kinds, and all the creatures that move along the ground according to their kinds. And God saw that it was good.

Then God said, "Let us make man in our image, in our likeness, and let them rule over the fish of the sea and the birds of the air, over the livestock, over all the earth, and over all the creatures that move along the ground."

So God created man in his own image,
in the image of God he created him;
male and female he created them.

God blessed them and said to them, "Be fruitful and increase in number; fill the earth and subdue it. Rule over the fish of the sea and the birds of the air and over every living creature that moves on the ground."

Then God said, "I give you every seed-bearing plant on the face of the whole earth and every tree that has fruit with seed in it. They will be yours for food. And to all the beasts of the earth and all the birds of the air and all the creatures that move on the ground—everything that has the breath of life in it—I give every green plant for food." And it was so.

God saw all that he had made, and it was very good. And there was evening, and there was morning—the sixth day.

Thus the heavens and the earth were completed in all their vast array. (Gen. 1:24–2:1)

God finishes the work of creation on the sixth day, filling the dry land with animals and then creating his image bearer for fellowship with him. First God creates various kinds of land animals, which seem to be divided into three wide types in contrast to the two types of vegetation and two types of fish. In a way parallel to the third day, here God pronounces the first part of his work on the sixth day—the creation of the land animals—to be good.

God then proceeds to the creation of man. God gives the fullest discussion to the creation of humankind of any of his acts of creation in Genesis 1. The focus is not on how man was created but the purpose and function of man. The first thing that we are told is that God made man in is own image and likeness. No other creature in Scripture bears that noble title and character. Man is uniquely blessed and privileged for the relationship and fellowship with God implied in bearing the image of God. The creation of man is the fulfillment of God's purpose in describing the six days of ordering God's creation. The words of blessing on the faithful in Psalm 115:14–16 expresses that truth: "May the LORD make you increase, both you and your children. May you be blessed by the LORD, the Maker of heaven and earth. The highest heavens belong to the LORD, but the earth he has given to man." The psalmist also celebrates man's rule on the earth in Psalm 8:6–8, "You made him ruler over the works of your hands; you put everything under his feet: all flocks and herds, and the beasts of the field, the birds of the air, and the fish of the sea, all that swim the paths of the seas."

In what way is man created in the image of God? A full answer to that question must be found in all of Scripture, and there we find that the image includes the moral and intellectual character of man. In the context of Genesis 1, however, the image is related immediately to the rule or dominion given to man over the fish of the sea, the birds of the air (stated twice: Gen. 1:26, 28), and over all the earth (stated only once in Gen. 1:26). Man is the culmination of creation and is like God in ruling.

Next the text declares that man, male and female, is made in the image of God. The sexual differences of various creatures are already implicit in the commission given to fish and birds to multiply and fill the earth. Here that difference is made explicit in reference to man to emphasize the equality of men and women as created in the image of God. That difference also provides the basis on which God will give man the commission to be fruitful and multiply.

The commission to multiply is the occasion for further description of the function of man: fill the earth, subdue it, and rule over it. This threefold mandate given to man is critical not only for understanding the work of man on earth but also to seeing the structure and meaning of Genesis 1 as a whole. These three elements of man's responsibility correspond to the three problems of Genesis 1:2 and to the ways in which God dealt with them. Man is to rule over the earth in a way analogous to God's sovereignty over the darkness. (We see clearly that God rules over the darkness by comparing days one and four. God shows his rule on day one by creating light—even though the word *rule* is not used there—because on day four he appoints the lights to rule over the day and night.) Man is to subdue the earth in a way analogous to the way God subdued the waters. Man is to fill the earth with his offspring in a way analogous to the way God filled creation with creatures. Man is to be a worker as God was a worker and so is indeed the image of God.

God has presented himself in the days of creation as a worker to be the model that man the worker will follow. As God needed to work to shape creation, so man will need to work. Man does not inherit a static world in which to be lazy. Man follows the pattern established by God of ruling, subduing, and filling. God has completed his work of creation, but man has much work yet to do. Even apart from sin, God intended man to work to develop creation from a simple garden to a wonderful city.

God also specifies that the vegetation is to be the food for man and for the animals. Here again the links between day three and day six are clear. These two days each have two distinct acts of creation and on the sixth day the land and vegetation of day three become the home and food of the land animals and humanity.

The day ends with God's final evaluation of his creation, including man. He finds it very good and complete. "Thus the heavens and the earth were completed in all their vast array" (Gen. 2:1). The problems of Genesis 1:2 are solved. The earth has light, dry land, and is full of the creatures God created. God has created man as his image bearer to have fellowship with him. The great work of creation is finished.

THE SEVENTH DAY

By the seventh day God had finished the work he had been doing; so on the seventh day he rested from all his work. And God
blessed the seventh day and made it holy, because on it he
rested from all the work of creating that he had done. (Gen.
2:2–4)

On the seventh day God, having finished his creation, rested from all his work. And because he had rested from all his work in creation on the seventh day, he blessed the seventh day and made it holy. These apparently simple words describing the seventh day show again the complex structure of the text. As Gordon Wenham summarized, "The threefold mention of the seventh day, each time in a sentence of seven Hebrew words, draws attention to the special character of the Sabbath. In this way form and content emphasize the distinctiveness of the seventh day."[12]

The presentation of the seventh day raises a number of questions that are vital to a correct understanding of Genesis 1. Three questions in particular will help us to understand the seventh day. Why is there no command for man to keep the Sabbath day holy? Why is the seventh day described differently from the other six days? What does it mean for God to rest? We will look at each of these questions in turn.

First, why is there no command for humanity to keep the Sabbath day holy? The absence of such a command has led some interpreters to conclude that God did not establish that day as a Sabbath for his people until he met with them at Mount Sinai. They argue that the Sabbath was not appointed at creation for all humankind but was a Mosaic institution only for Israel as a nation. But such an approach ignores a number of scriptural teachings. The Israelites kept the Sabbath holy before they came to Sinai (Ex. 16). The patriarchs observed a seven-day week. And most significantly, a covenantal reading of Genesis 1 shows us that a command is implicit in the description of the seventh day.

A covenantal approach recognizes that the seventh day, like all the revelation of Genesis 1, is for the people of God. The Israelites, when reading Genesis to find out where they had come from, would have read Genesis 2:2–3 and said, "There is the origin of our Sabbath." There was no need to command observance of the Sabbath in Genesis 2, since the Israelites would already have known that they were obligated to observe it. The creation story tells them where their practice came from: not just from Sinai but from creation. God had taught them this truth in the Ten Commandments, Exodus 20:8–11, "Remember the Sabbath day by keeping it holy. . . . For in six days the LORD made the heavens and earth, the sea, and all that is in them, but he rested on the seventh day."

It is surely ironic that many people today who most insistently claim that it is obvious that the days of Genesis 1 are ordinary twenty-four-hour days miss the most important point about the days, namely, that one day in seven is holy to the Lord. They deny that the Sabbath is grounded in creation and maintain that it is a Mosaic institution that passed away with the coming of Christ. But when we remember that Genesis is covenant history, we know that one of the most important teachings of Genesis 1 is that the Sabbath is part of the created order and a perpetual obligation for humankind.[13]

The second question to consider about the seventh day is, Why is the seventh day described differently from the other six days? Obviously God does not create on this day, but also the acts of creation are not reiterated as they were on the other days, and God does not declare the day good as he did with all of the other days except day two. Most striking perhaps is that we find no reference to evening and morning on that day.

Some interpreters, particularly those who take the framework interpretation, have speculated that there is no evening and morning on the seventh day because on that day God entered into his eternal rest. This interpretation usually appeals for support to Hebrews 4 and its teaching about an everlasting Sabbath that God now enjoys and that yet awaits the people of God. But such an approach changes the seventh day into something radically different from the other days. It also seems to assume what it needs to prove in relation to Hebrews 4. There we are told that God rested on the seventh day and we are told that God is resting now. But we are not told that the seventh day itself is everlasting. Hebrews 4 is not exegeting Genesis 2:2–3 but is interpreting Psalm 95. When God promises that the unbelieving will not enter his rest, he is speaking more of the promised land as rest than of the Sabbath day.

As we will see more fully later, the best explanation for the absence of evening and morning on the seventh day is again as a pointer that the meaning of the days of Genesis 1 is not so obvious as some people believe and that we must search carefully to find their meaning for us. Moses intended that we should wonder, If God rested on the seventh day, and the days of creation are ordinary days, then did God begin to work again on the eighth day? Understanding God's rest is critical for understanding Genesis 1.

For the interpretation of Genesis 1 as a whole, then, the third question is the most important: What does it mean for God to rest? The question is even more focused for us by the language of Exodus 31:17, "on the seventh day he rested and was refreshed"(ESV).[14] The word *refreshed* in Hebrew can even mean "caught his breath." Exodus 23:12 uses this word of people as they recover from fatigue: "Six days do your work, but on the seventh day do not work, so that your ox and your donkey may rest and the slave born in your household, and the alien as well, may be refreshed."[15] Are Genesis 1 and Exodus 31 saying God was tired after his work and in need of rest? Was God weary and in need of refreshment? Such conclusions are not only impossible; they are blasphemous. God is the eternal, immutable, and impassable one. No amount of creative work could tire him.

Various explanations of this rest have been made. Calvin suggested that God's rest was a ceasing from his creative work but not from his work in providence. That is possible. But that explanation would not explain the reference to God being refreshed.

To understand this rest we need to reflect also on the words of Jesus in John 5. When Jesus was criticized for healing on the Sabbath, he defended himself by saying, "My Father is always at his work to this very day, and I, too, am working" (John 5:17). The clear point of his argument is that the Father did work on the Sabbath just as Jesus had worked. Jesus is saying that God did not rest on the Sabbath.

If God cannot need rest and refreshment and if Jesus tells us that God did not rest on the Sabbath, then what is the meaning of the Sabbath day? We can only conclude that God spoke about himself as he does in Genesis 2 in order to teach us about ourselves. If we are his image, then he presents his rest so that we can know about our own. He does not need to rest, but we do. He is accommodating his revelation of his creating work to us and our needs. He speaks of himself in a way that serves as a model for us.

Jesus understood the Father as his model when he spoke of the Father working on the Sabbath: "I tell you the truth, the Son can do nothing by himself; he can do only what he sees his Father doing, because whatever the Father does the Son also does" (John 5:19). Here Jesus—the second Adam, the true man, the ultimate image bearer of God— shows that he and all people are to base their lives on the pattern they see in God.

3

THE MESSAGE OF GENESIS 1

N
ow that we have looked closely at the text of Genesis 1, we must ask what conclusions we should draw about the proper meaning of that passage. The passage is rich in complexity, both in its literary form and its detailed content. Moses under the inspiration of the Holy Spirit constructed this introduction to the Book of Genesis with great care and purpose. We need to look at it with equal care to grasp the message that Moses intended. We should not be surprised that understanding the ways of God in creation is not easy. As God said to Job, "Where were you when I laid the earth's foundation? Tell, me, if you understand" (Job 38:4).

BIBLE, GOD, AND CREATION

To reach the meaning of Genesis 1, we need to review what the Bible tells us generally about God as he reveals himself to us. The Bible reveals God using images and forms that do not exhaustively describe God as he is in himself but present him in relation to us in words and comparisons accommodated to our understanding. For example, Isaiah 59:16 says of God, "his own arm worked salvation for him." What does the Bible mean when it speaks of the arm of God? Are we to believe that God has a physical body to which is attached a physical arm? The church has always and rightly rejected such a wooden reading of the text. We know that the arm of God is a metaphor in which God uses a human image to describe his strength and his activity. Describing God in such human forms is called anthropomorphism, from the Greek meaning "human form."

Such forms of speech are also found in Genesis 1, as we have already seen. When we read that "God said," we know that God does not have a mouth. We know that it is an expression of God's creative powers. When we read that God saw that something was good, does that mean that he has eyes or that he went through a deliberative process? No, both expressions record the pleasure that God took in his creation. God is revealing himself using human terms to describe his work so that human beings would understand his revelation.

Similarly the Scriptures often use metaphorical language for God as if he existed in space, even though we know that God is spirit and does not occupy space. The Bible often presents heaven as the abode of God (e.g., Psalm 2:4, "The One enthroned in heaven"). But God does not exist only in some localized place.

We also know that the Bible describes God as appearing visibly as well as occupying space. Those appearances, however, do not describe him as he is in himself but reveal something of his character and his relationship with his people through a visible form. For example, God meets with Moses in the burning bush: "There the angel of the LORD appeared to him in the flames of fire from within a bush. Moses saw that though the bush was on fire it did not burn up. . . . When the LORD saw that he had gone over to look, God called to him from within the bush, 'Moses! Moses!' " (Ex. 3:2, 4). God represents himself as a bush that is burning or as an angel within the bush. He does that for the sake of Moses to teach him something of the nature of his relationship with his people: a people who have suffered but have not been consumed because their God has protected them. Moses truly sees a bush and an angel, but he has not seen God as he is in himself. He has seen a visible representation of the presence and care of the Lord. The angel in particular shows his care: "In all their distress he too was distressed, and the angel of his presence saved them" (Isa. 63:9).

Another such visible appearance is God's enthronement between the wings of the cherubim over the mercy seat of the ark of the covenant: "they brought back the ark of the covenant of the LORD Almighty, who is enthroned between the cherubim" (1 Sam. 4:4). Does God sit above the mercy seat? Israel saw a manifestation of glory there between the wings of the cherubim (compare Ex. 25:22; 40:34). But that place is not the only location where God is present. Rather God in the appearance of his glory above the mercy seat is revealing that in his fellowship with his people he does not judge them in light of the broken law but in light of his mercy symbolized in the atoning work of his priests.

Another such appearance is God's revelation of himself to Isaiah: "I saw the LORD seated on a throne, high and exalted, and the train of his robe filled the temple" (Isa. 6:1). Does God sit on a throne and have glorious robes that he wears? No, he revealed himself in that way to show Isaiah his power and holiness, which Isaiah was to preach to Israel.

As the Bible frequently presents God as occupying space even though he is spirit, so the Bible often presents God as in time even though he exists beyond time. He is called the Ancient of Days (Dan. 7:9), not to say that he is old but to say that he is eternal. That point is also made in Psalm 90:4, "For a thousand years in your sight are like a day that has just gone by, or like a watch in the night." The psalmist is not teaching that a day and a thousand years are interchangeable in the Bible or that time goes by really quickly for God. Rather he is teaching that God lives above time in eternity.

The Bible uses these literary forms and metaphors with particular frequency in certain styles of writing. In poetry such as the Psalms we expect and easily recognize such forms. In prophecy we also see such usage, although it may not always be easy to see when God is speaking metaphorically. For example, consider the great prophecy of the future in Isaiah 65. In Isaiah 65:17 God declares that he will create a new heaven and a new earth, and we naturally understand that as referring to the final state of blessedness described as a new heaven and a new earth in Revelation 21. But Isaiah goes on to say, "He who dies at a hundred will be thought a mere youth" (Isa. 65:20). In Isaiah 65 either the new heaven and the new earth of verse 17 or the man dying of verse 20 must be seen as metaphorical. The best solution seems to be that Isaiah is describing the final state of the creation but using images that we know well in order to help us to see it. We do not know what living forever means, but we easily know what it means to live to a very old age. So Isaiah uses familiar language as a metaphor to teach us about a kind of life that we have never experienced.

What is true of poetry and prophecy may well be true of the account of creation in Genesis 1 as well. After all, we have no real experience of that phenomenon of creation at the beginning of time. We know the world only as a created, functioning, purposeful place. In order to tell us about creation, God uses images and language that we can understand. But much of the language must be figurative.

Recognizing metaphors and anthropomorphic expressions for God should help us be clear about what a literal interpretation of the Bible means. Properly the literal interpretation of a text takes the words of the text to mean what the text intended them to mean. To return to our example of the arm of God (Isa. 59), is the literal reading of the text that God has a physical arm or that the arm is a metaphor for the strength of God? Clearly the literal meaning of the text is the metaphorical interpretation. To believe that God has a physical arm is not the literal interpretation of the text but a wooden, crass interpretation. So the literal meaning of Genesis 1 is the meaning that Moses intended—whether that turns out to be the traditional understanding or one of the figurative interpretations.

We know that the Bible uses literary forms and metaphors frequently in speaking of God. But they are also common in biblical reflections on creation. Consider Job 38:5–10, where God speaks of his work of creation:

Who marked off its dimensions? Surely you know! Who stretched a measuring line across it? On what were its footings set, or who laid its cornerstone—while the morning stars sang together and all the angels shouted for joy? Who shut up the sea behind doors when it burst forth from the womb, when I made the clouds its garment and wrapped it in thick darkness, when I fixed limits for it and set its doors and bars in place . . . ?

Over and over Job in this brief text uses literary figures of speech: for example, a measuring line, footings, cornerstone, morning stars singing, the doors, and womb of the sea. The literal meaning of the text is not that God used a measuring line in his work of creation but that he set the dimensions of the world.

Our review of some of the many places in which the Bible uses human terms, human space, and human time to describe God, particularly in his work of creation, should help us to see that Genesis 1 describes God's work in language that at many points describes a human worker. God makes the world as man makes the products of his hands. Of course we see also the great difference between man and God: God creates out of nothing by the word of his power while man forms materials that already exist by his hands. Still the picture of God in Genesis 1 is in many ways anthropomorphic. Notice, for example, that after the creation of daylight God seems always to work during the day, not during the night. God's work by day may well be described in this way to serve as a model to man in his working. Think of Psalm 104—a great psalm about creation that reminds us that God "wraps himself in light as with a garment" (Ps. 104:2). That psalm does present man as a worker by day and may suggest a parallel between the work of God in creation and the work of man day by day.[1] The psalmist wrote: "You bring darkness, it becomes night, and all the beasts of the forest prowl. The lions roar for their prey and seek their food from God. The sun rises, and they steal away; they return and lie down in their dens. Then man goes out to his work, to his labor until evening" (Ps. 104:20–23). Man's labor during the day is the image or reflection of what God did in Genesis 1.

BIBLE, TIME, AND CREATION

The story of Genesis 1 is a telling of the creative work of God in a form that we can understand. Part of the form that God uses to communicate with us is through familiar units of time, namely, days and a week.

How does Genesis use the word *day* in its early verses? That question is important since the days of creation are the most apparent part of the structure Moses gave to the introduction of Genesis. It is also important since many people today argue that it is obvious that the word *day* must mean a twenty-four-hour day in Genesis 1. We need to see that the word *day* is used in as many as seven different ways in the short space of Genesis 1:1–2:4. First, "day" in Genesis 1:5 means daylight—in our experience twelve hours, not twenty-four hours. Second, later in that same verse "day" means the whole day of evening and morning, apparently twenty-four hours long. Third, the first three days of Genesis 1—at least according to the traditional interpretation—are distinct as presolar days.[2] We cannot know with certainty how long such days would be. Fourth, the solar days after the creation of the sun are another use of the word *day*. Fifth, the seventh day of Genesis 2:1–3 is at least described differently from the other days in that evening and morning are not mentioned in relation to it. Sixth, in Hebrew the numerals for the sixth and seventh days are preceded by the definite article, whereas there are no definite articles preceding the numerals for the other days.[3] This shift from "day five" to "the day six" and "the day seven" is another way in which Moses highlighted the importance of those days in the text. Finally, and significantly, Genesis 2:4 as the first verse of the first of the generations of Genesis reads: "These are the generations of the heavens and the earth when they were created, in the day that the LORD God made the earth and the heavens."[4] Here the word *day* stands for the whole period of the creative activity of God. This use of "day" is particularly significant because it shows that in summarizing the work of creation at the beginning of the first of the generations in Genesis, Moses says the creation took place in a day.[5]

When we consider these different usages of the word *day* and remember that the summary of creation in Genesis 1:1 does not refer to six days, we surely need to ponder exactly what Moses intends to teach us here about the days of creation. Are these all indicators that the precise meaning of the six days is not quite so obvious as many claim? Moses seems by his varied usage of "day" to suggest something more than a simple chronology of God's actions.

Why then does God use seven days in his account of creation? Why does God spread the words of creation, which he speaks in just a few minutes, over six days? The key answer is that he uses seven days to reveal the week that will be a fundamental part of the rhythm of human life. He is not showing us exactly the time he took to create but is revealing to us the way in which the seven-day week will order our lives as his people. We learn to divide our time into weeks, not from nature but only from revelation. The seven-day week is not grounded in the rhythms of the physical world as the day, the month, and the year are. The week rests on the revelation of God to his image bearer by which God shows man how in all his living he is to follow the model that God has presented. Man is to work six days and rest one day every week.

From this complete week of God's creation and man's work and rest, seven becomes the number of completeness or perfection in the Bible (see Gen. 4:15, 24; Lev. 26:18–28; and Ps. 79:12 as examples of seven used as the number of completeness). This significance for the number seven in creation leads to seven being used as a symbol of the completion of history in the apocalyptic books, Daniel (chap. 9) and the Revelation of John. In the Revelation the number seven is used over and over again: seven spirits, seven churches, seven lamps, seven stars, seven angels, seven seals, seven horns, seven eyes, seven trumpets, seven thunders, seven heads, seven crowns, seven plagues, seven bowls, seven hills, and seven kings. In particular, the seven trumpets (Rev. 8:6–11:19) at several points seem to echo the creation story as they mark the wrath of God falling on the earth, the sea, and the sun, moon, and stars.

We should not be surprised that a chronological unit would be used in the Bible to mean something more than just a measurement of time. We have already seen such usage in our discussions of Matthew's genealogy and of the thousand years in Revelation 20. Here in Genesis 1 we see again a chronological term—*day*—that has a different function and meaning than the obvious.

THE FIRST THREE GENERATIONS

The interpretation of Genesis 1 that we are proposing in this study is strengthened when we look carefully at the first three generations of the Book of Genesis (Gen. 2:4–9:29). The exact relationship of these sections of Genesis requires careful examination. They will help us in our consideration of how we should understand the chronological sequence presented in Genesis 1. They will also reinforce the centrality of man as created in the image of God for the opening chapters of Genesis.

The first of the generations is "the generations of the heavens and the earth" (Gen. 2:4–4:26). This section is particularly important because in part it retells the story of creation and raises important issues on the matter of historical sequence. Liberal critics of the Bible have claimed that there are two contradictory accounts of creation in the early chapters of Genesis because the order of the events of creation is different in the two accounts. But such a criticism misses the purpose of these early chapters. Genesis 1 presents creation as the progressive ordering of the earth to be a home for man in fellowship with God and to teach man how he is to bear God's image. Genesis 2:4–4:26 begins with the creation of man in fellowship with God and then presents the formation of a place for people to live. The story then goes on to trace man's violation of that fellowship and the way in which God begins to restore that fellowship. These are not contradictory accounts but accounts of the same acts of creation from different perspectives for different purposes.

The traditional interpretation of Genesis 1 relates the two accounts of creation by teaching that Genesis 1 is the chronological account while Genesis 2 should be harmonized to agree with it. This harmonization is usually achieved by treating several of the verbs in Genesis 2 as pluperfect in tense. The NIV translation follows this approach, for example, in Genesis 2:5 and Genesis 2:8, "and no shrub of the field had yet appeared on the earth and no plant of the field had yet sprung up, for the LORD God had not sent rain on the earth and there was no man to work the ground. . . . Now the LORD God had planted a garden in the east, in Eden; and there he put the man he had formed." The translation of these verbs as pluperfect places the creation of the vegetation and the garden before the creation of man and so harmonizes Genesis 1 and Genesis 2.

Such a harmonization of Genesis 1 and Genesis 2 is possible but not obvious. On the surface Genesis 2 and its verbs are just as simple and straightforward a chronology as Genesis 1. The apparent chronology of Genesis 2 is as follows: on the one day in which God created the earth and the heavens (Gen 2:4) God first created man. At that time no plant had yet been created. Then God created plants. After that God created animals and birds. And then God created woman. Look at a more literal and natural translation of key verses in Genesis 2 (Gen. 2:4, 5, 7, 18, 19, 22):

> These are the generations of the heavens and the earth when they were created, in the day that the LORD God made earth and the heavens. When no bush of the field was yet in the land and no small plant of the field had yet sprung up—for the LORD God had not caused it to rain on the land, . . . then the LORD God formed the man of dust from the ground. . . . Then the LORD God said, 'It is not good that the man should be alone; I will make him a helper fit for him. So out of the ground the LORD God formed every beast of the field and every bird of the heavens and brought them to the man to see what he would call them. . . . And the rib that the LORD God had taken from the man he made into a woman. (ESV)

If we follow the more natural translation of Genesis 2 from the English Standard Version, how do we correlate the two accounts of creation? To answer that question we must look with care at these accounts, reflecting on the similarities and the differences in the first three chapters of Genesis.

The openings of the accounts are quite similar. Look at word-for-word translations (see Fig. 7).

Fig. 7. Translations of Genesis 1:1–2 and 2:4

Genesis 1:1–2	In beginning created God the heavens and the earth. And the earth. . . .
Genesis 2:4	These generations of the heavens and the earth when they were created in day made Yahweh God earth and heavens. . . .

In both God creates the heavens and the earth. In both earth then becomes the focus of God's activity. In both we have rather parallel constructions: "in beginning" and "in day." The differences are primarily between the words "the beginning" and "the day" and between using the simple reference to God and then adding his covenant name, Yahweh.

In both accounts the primary focus is on the creation of man and the making of a dwelling suitable for man. Both also focus on man as bearing the image of God. The language of image is not used in the second account, but the exercise of the image and the betrayal of the image are the central themes.

The differences between the two accounts help us to see the different purposes of the two accounts. In Genesis 1

man is the last act of creation showing that man is the culmination of creation. In Genesis 2 man is the first act of creation showing that man is the prime focus of creation.
They both in their different ways show that man is central
to God's creation. Genesis 1 gives man the mandate of
what it means to bear the image of God. Genesis 2 and
Genesis 3 show man exercising the responsibilities of the
image and then betraying the image in yielding to temptation. Genesis 1 gives a broader account of creation, telling
of the creation of light, the lights, the seas, and the fish, all
of which are missing in the second account. Genesis 2 and
Genesis 3 give a more specific and detailed account of the
creation of humanity.

The detailed focus on man in Genesis 2 and Genesis 3
has several elements. God creates man from the dust of the
earth and gives him the breath of life. He makes a garden
and places the man in it. He tells us the name of the garden and the rivers that water it. He commands the man to
care for the garden and not to eat from one tree lest he die.
God forms all the animals and birds out of the ground and
brings them to the man to name and to see if he could find
a suitable helper. God then creates the woman from
Adam's rib. In his working and naming and marrying
Adam is fulfilling his calling as the image of God. He rules
and subdues and fills.

The evil one then comes to tempt Eve and Adam, rais-
ing questions about what it means to be the image of God.
He suggests that they will be "like God" (Gen. 3:5) if they
eat from the forbidden tree and gain a knowledge of good
and evil. The devil's contention is a lie. They already know

good and will not be improved by knowing evil. They are already like God in the best possible way. But in yielding to this temptation they betray and corrupt the image of God in them. Adam, who should have subdued the evil one through obedience, allows himself to be subdued by the devil.

Then God comes in judgment for this temptation and sin, showing himself as the good and righteous model that Adam should have emulated. In judgment first, God subdues the serpent, cursing him to go upon his belly (Gen. 3:14) humbled before God. He also declares that one day the seed of the woman as the second and true Adam will come to be the faithful image bearer of God and will subdue the serpent, finally and completely crushing his head (Gen. 3:15). Second, God curses the woman for her betrayal of God and his gift of the image in her. God curses her in her childbearing through which she was to fill the earth. He curses her also in her relationship with her husband where she should have accepted his loving rule over her (Gen. 3:16). Third, God curses the man in a similar way. Where Adam should have ruled over and subdued the earth, now the earth will weary him and bring forth weeds as well as wheat (Gen. 3:17–19). As the man and the woman were created to live in blessed, joyful service and fellowship with God, now they will experience alienation, frustration, and death. They are driven from the garden and from the tree of life. To underscore their loss God ironically comments that they have become like him (Gen. 3:22)! Sin increases in human experience (Gen. 4:24) and over some of their descendents sin comes to dominate completely (e.g., Gen. 4:7).

This judgment, however, does not destroy the purpose of man in God's creation. Man even as a sinner still has work to do in the service of God (see Gen. 4:20–21). God also preserves a people who desire to fellowship with him in worship (Gen. 4:26). God's plan for creation and for redemption will not fail. He has promised to send a Savior who will withstand the temptations of the evil one, rule in righteousness, subdue his enemies, and fill the world with his spiritual offspring (Isa. 53:10).

The central place given to man as the image bearer of God in Genesis 1 and in the first generation of the Book of Genesis continues in generations two (Gen. 5:1–6:8) and three (Gen. 6:9–9:29). The second generation—the generations of Adam—begins: "When God created man, he made him in the likeness of God. He created them male and female and blessed them. And when they were created, he called them 'man.' When Adam had lived 130 years, he had a son in his own likeness, in his own image; and he named him Seth" (Gen. 5:1–3). Here the image of God is linked to man's mission to fill the earth with his own offspring. As God had created Adam in his image, so Adam fathers Seth in his image. The discussion of the image focuses on Seth rather than Cain, because it is through Seth that the blessings of the covenant of grace pass. Seth rather than Cain is truly manifesting the image of God as the one who fellowships with God.

Although God preserves his image in humankind, the reality of the fallen and cursed world also continues. Noah is given a name that sounds like the Hebrew word for comfort, because as his father, Lamech, said, "He will comfort us in the labor and painful toil of our hands caused by the ground the LORD has cursed" (Gen. 5:29). But the growing willfulness and evil of humankind grieves the Lord, and he determines to bring a destructive judgment on his creatures (Gen. 6:2, 5–7).

In generation three—the generations of Noah—this judgment is carried out. People have filled the world, not with the goodness that God intended from the beginning but with evil and violence: "Now the earth was corrupt in God's sight and was full of violence. God saw how corrupt the earth had become, for all the people on earth had corrupted their ways" (Gen. 6:11–12). God's judgment will in a sense undo creation. The waters that had been subdued will now be released to destroy all living creatures: "I am going to bring floodwaters on the earth to destroy all life under the heavens, every creature that has the breath of life" (Gen. 6:17). It was not just rain that destroyed the world. "All the springs of the great deep burst forth, and the floodgates of the heavens opened" (Gen. 7:11).

Even in this terrible judgment the Lord preserves a people for his name (the family of Noah) and a few animals for the new world after the flood. After the waters receded and the earth was dry again, God renews and extends his covenant with humankind in the person of Noah. He reiterates man's responsibilities as the image bearer of God: "Be fruitful and increase in number and fill the earth" (Gen. 9:1). God orders protection for man: "Whoever sheds the blood of man, by man shall his blood be shed; for in the image of God has God made man" (Gen. 9:6).

In the subsequent generations of the Book of Genesis Moses tells us how in the midst of sin and corruption God preserves a covenant people from whom a Savior of the world would come. God promised in Genesis 3 that the seed of the woman would crush the head of the serpent. In Genesis 12 he promises Abram that all the nations of the earth will be blessed through his descendents. The focus on the image of God that begins in Genesis culminates in the coming of Jesus, who is the true and faithful image of God and Savior of his people.

We have taken a rather careful look at these generations in order to seen how central man as God's image bearer is in the story of Genesis. These subsequent generations help us to realize that we should not be surprised to find that the real purpose of Genesis 1 is to tell us about the way people are to be like God.

These generations also should give us pause as we think of the matter of chronological sequence. In generations two through ten in the Book of Genesis, Moses tells his stories in a straightforward chronological sequence. It seems most likely then that we should expect the first generation also to follow a similar kind of sequence. Genesis 1, as the introduction to the generations of the rest of the book, could well be organized in some way other than simple chronology. We should see that however one resolves the apparent chronologies of Genesis 1 and Genesis 2, God's primary concern in both accounts is not to give us a specific chronology of God's acts but to show us

God's meaning and purpose for humanity in creation. Our covenantal approach shows that revelatory purpose clearly.

TRADITIONAL INTERPRETATION PROBLEMS

Our study to this point has uncovered a number of problems that exist for the traditional interpretation with its notion that God acted to create in six twenty-four-hour days. First, only three of the seven days of Genesis 1 are described as normal days, namely, with a sun to shine and an evening and morning. Second, the traditional view does not explain the identities between day one and day four presented in the text. Third, this view creates a conflict between Genesis 1, where the vegetation is created before man, while in Genesis 2:6 man seems to be created before the vegetation. Fourth, this view cannot easily account for the absence of the statement "And God saw that it was good" in day two. Fifth, this view, insisting as it does that the meaning of "day" in Genesis 1 is obviously a twenty-four-hour day, creates a contradiction between Genesis 1 and Genesis 2:4, where we are told that the whole creation occurred in a day.

Defenders of the traditional view make two claims for their interpretation that we have not yet explored. First, they maintain that the use of "and" in the Hebrew text of Genesis 1 (the *waw* consecutive) followed by the past tense suggests a chronological sequence in the text. But that use of "and" is not always sequential in Genesis 1. The "and" at the beginning of Genesis 1:16 is clearly not sequential unless God creates the lights twice.[6]

Second, defenders of the traditional view make another argument repeatedly and forcefully. They insist that church history is nearly unanimously on their side.[7] They are correct that the vast majority of historical interpretation of Genesis 1 is traditional. Still a figurative interpretation is present in the history of the church, defended by such notables as Clement of Alexandria (late second to early third century), Augustine (fifth century), Anselm (eleventh century), Peter Lombard (twelfth century), and perhaps the young Thomas Aquinas (thirteenth century). Because some excellent minds in the history of the church who were not liberals or influenced by modern science did not see the meaning of the days of Genesis 1 as obviously twenty-four-hour hours, perhaps everyone should be careful of making such a claim. We need to remember that in the history of the church the vast majority of interpreters of the Bible were wrong for centuries on certain issues. Until the seventeenth century, the vast majority of interpreters thought that the Bible clearly taught that the earth was at the center of the universe. Until the sixteenth century, almost all interpreters taught an erroneous view of justification. The vast majority of interpreters have been seriously wrong on a number of obvious issues in the history of the church.

As Protestants, we do not attribute authority to the tradition of the church. Only the Bible is our authority, and we know the meaning of the Bible only by letting it interpret itself as we compare text with text. In this regard the way in which the Bible characteristically speaks of God's creation is very important. We find extensive reflection on creation in Job, the Psalms, and Isaiah, as well as other parts of the Bible. In none of these reflections on creation is there any reference to the "days" of creation. These sections celebrate the great creative work of God but without use anywhere of the creation days.

Job 38 is an especially good case of such reflection on creation. God is instructing Job to face his limitations through a series of questions related to creation. God points to the creation of the earth (Job 38:4, 6), setting boundaries to the sea (Job 38:8, 10–11), shaping clouds (Job 38;9), and making the day (Job 38:12). Here Job alludes to God's work on the first three days of Genesis 1, but Job makes no reference to the days themselves. Indeed Job 38:14 gives a wonderful statement of what creation was: "The earth takes shape like clay under a seal." In creation God is shaping a world for man to teach him how to live as the image bearer of God.

It is remarkable in light of the stress that some place on the importance of twenty-four-hour days that outside of Genesis 1 there are only two references to the days of creation in the Bible. The first reference is in Proverbs 8:

"I was there when he set the heavens in place,
     when he marked out the horizon on the face of
          the deep,
when he established the clouds above
     and fixed securely the fountains of the deep,
when he gave the sea its boundary

> so the waters would not overstep his command,
> and when he marked out the foundations of the
> earth.
> Then I was the craftsman at his side.
> I was filled with delight day after day, rejoicing al-
> ways in his presence,
> rejoicing in his whole world
> and delighting in mankind." (Prov. 8:27–31)

In this poetic celebration of creation the speaker is Wisdom, an attribute of God personified as a woman. She is
the architect-craftsman assisting the divine builder. She is
clearly contrasted with folly, who is represented as an
adulterous woman. Here Wisdom is rejoicing particularly
in the creation of the sky, the seas, and the land, which are
the creative works of days two and three in Genesis 1. As
wisdom surveys this work "day after day," she delights in
God and in the man he has made. Here the days mentioned are part of a metaphorical, poetic meditation on creation. No clear reference is made to days two and three of
Genesis 1. Rather Wisdom seems to be contemplating creation over many days. The reference to days here tends if
anything to reinforce our interpretation that the days of
Genesis 1 are not a strict chronology of God's acts.

The second set of references to the days of creation outside of Genesis 1 concerns the Sabbath commandment (Ex.
20:11; 31:17).[8] As we have seen, the command for man to
rest one day in seven depends on the creation account of
Genesis 1. But this command also fits precisely with the
covenantal view of the days of creation that we have been

developing. All of the pieces of revelation in the Bible about creation support our contention that the days of Genesis 1 are intended to teach man about his working and resting as a mirror of God.

GOD, CREATION, AND MAN

All of our considerations of the Bible's teaching on days and time should lead us to the conclusion that the days and week of Genesis 1 are presented to us as a real week of twenty-four-hour days. These days and week, however, do not describe God's actions in themselves but present God's creative purpose in a way that is a model for us. The purpose and message of Genesis 1 is that God created the world for humankind—a world in which man could be the image of God in his working and his resting.

Does this conclusion mean, however, that the week of creation is not a literal description of the work of God? Our covenantal approach has shown that Moses did not record an abstract chronology of God's actions. He rather presented the creative work of God in a chronological pattern for us. As God is the builder so we are to build. As God rests, so we are to rest. The days were created for us, not for God, who always dwells above time in eternity. This covenantal interpretation is a literal interpretation for it has sought to follow Moses in his own terms. It is also historical in its approach as it affirms that God created in time and by his sovereign power everything described in Genesis 1.

Still the question may remain: Does this covenantal interpretation mean that God did not do what Genesis 1 says he did? No, indeed! God is the Creator who really created—not only light and sea and land, lights and animals and man, but also the week that patterns the lives of his image bearers.

Some people will still object that on this reading Genesis 1 tells us only what and why God created, not how he created. Our first response is that the text does tell us how he created, namely, by his great power and will. But we would also observe that the early chapters of Genesis show us that Genesis 1 is not about the details of how God created. Remember that Genesis 1 presents the creation of people as a direct exercise of God's power: "Then God said, 'Let us make man. . . . ' So God created man" (Gen. 1:26–27). How did God create man? It appears as we read these words that God created man out of nothing by the word of his power. But in Genesis 2:7 we read, "The LORD God formed the man from the dust of the ground and breathed into his nostrils the breath of life, and the man became a living being." Genesis 1 tells us ultimately how God created man, namely, by the word of his power. But Genesis 2 tells us more specifically how God made man, namely, from the dust of the earth. Although Genesis 1 tells us something of how God created man, it tells us more fully the purpose of God in creating man. So Genesis 1 as a whole focuses not so much on how God made the world for man but on the meaning, purpose, and order of that creation for man.

We have interpreted Genesis 1 to mean that in creation God has revealed himself as a model to his people through a description of himself in terms of actions that are meant to be understood figuratively. We will appreciate this interpretation more if we see that God reveals himself in exactly this way in other historical parts of the Bible. Consider Exodus 12:42, "Because the LORD kept vigil that night to bring them out of Egypt, on this night all Israelites are to keep vigil to honor the LORD for the generations to come." Here Moses presents the Lord's action of keeping vigil as a model and pattern for the Israelites to follow. But did the Lord really keep vigil? Was he more attentive that night than on other nights? Is not the Lord always watching and caring for his people with equal attention? Clearly the image of the Lord being especially on guard one night is not describing him as he is in himself but is teaching us of his care and is serving as a model and pattern for Israel to follow.[9]

Another such example comes from the story of the tower of Babel. There sinful men in their pride set out to build a tower to reach to heaven (Gen. 11:4). The Bible then gives us God's response: "But the LORD came down to see the city and the tower that the men were building" (Gen. 11:5). Did God need to travel to see what was happening in Babel? Of course not! God knows all things and sees all things without travel or effort. He reveals himself as coming down to show us how puny the efforts of those sinners really were and to teach us humility before our God. He presents himself as traveling from heaven to show us how far from heaven the tower was. He is not telling us about himself as he is. He is showing us his majesty in this language of coming down. We see the same message in Psalm 113:5–6: "Who is like the LORD our God, the One who sits enthroned on high, who stoops down to look on the heavens and the earth?"

Another parallel biblical example will help illumine our approach to the creation story. That example is the heavenly temple. We are told that God instructed Moses on the details of how to build the tabernacle and everything in it, saying, "See that you make them according to the pattern shown you on the mountain" (Ex. 25:40). The Lord also gave David specifics for the plan for the temple: " 'All this,' David said, 'I have in writing from the hand of the LORD upon me, and he gave me understanding in all the details of the plan' " (1 Chron. 28:19). The Book of Hebrews develops this theme of divine instruction about the building of the temple. Of the Old Testament priests we read, "They serve at a sanctuary that is a copy and shadow of what is in heaven" (Heb. 8:5). Further, Hebrews teaches that the ascended Christ now "serves in the sanctuary, the true tabernacle set up by the Lord, not by man" (Heb. 8:2). Hebrews repeatedly refers to the heavenly temple as the model of the earthly. But what is the nature of that heavenly temple? Is it physical? Does God have a material dwelling in heaven? No. The heavenly temple is a revelation to us and for us to help us understand something of the character of heaven, a spiritual reality. It is a heavenly model, pattern, and reality, not for God but for our instruction.

When we get to heaven, we will not see a temple. Rather we will see God. The heavenly temple stands for the reality, holiness, blessedness, and intimacy of our meeting with God in heaven. Is the heavenly temple real? Yes, as God's instruction about how to build the earthly temple and about what blessed fellowship with God awaits us. Notice how Hebrews passes from the idea of the heavenly temple to heaven in this statement: "Christ did not enter a man-made sanctuary that was only a copy of the true one; he entered heaven itself, now to appear for us in God's presence" (Heb. 9:24). The heavenly temple is real as a model for us, not as a heavenly dwelling that God needs.

Just as the heavenly temple is real as a revelation of heaven, so the account of creation is real as a revelation of the Creator and his work. The creation account is given to us in terms that we can understand to instruct us in the way that we should live in light of God's purpose for us in creation.

How then can we summarize what Genesis 1 is teaching us? First, we see that Genesis 1 is the foundation of our covenantal relationship with God. God is the great Creator of all things who created the earth as the place in which he would have fellowship with humanity. God structures the creation for man as his covenant image bearer. The pattern of creation reveals that people are to work for God six days and rest in fellowship with God one day each week.

Second, we see that Moses has constructed an intricate literary text in Genesis 1. That intricate structure draws us into the text to study it with the greatest care. In that study we see how Moses used various figurative forms to show us what God did. Those forms point us to the meaning of the text. The days show the progressive way in which God solved the three problems of Genesis 1:2 to make the earth habitable for humankind. Moses highlights the importance of the fourth day by repeating several times the function of the lights. He shows how the creation culminates in the creation of man, not only by making man the last act of creation but also by devoting so much space to describing the mandate that God gives to man.

Third, we see that the days of Genesis 1 are ordinary, twenty-four-hour days. But many pointers indicate that these ordinary days are for us as a model for our working, not as a time schedule that God followed. Those pointers include the character of God's rest on the seventh day, the identity of functions for the light and the lights uniting the first and fourth days, and the various ways in which the word *day* is used, particularly in Genesis 2:4. The days are actual for us but figurative for God. They are not a timetable of God's actions but are a model timetable for us to follow.

CONTROVERSY TODAY

Near the beginning of this study we noted that a great deal of controversy has arisen over the interpretation of Genesis 1 in the last decade or so. Why has that happened? It is not the result of new discoveries of modern science that present new challenges to the Bible. It is also not the result of new discoveries in the interpretation of the Bible that strengthen the ordinary day approach. So why has the controversy intensified and become so strident? It appears to be the result of a heightened sense of alienation from our dominant culture that conservative Christians have come to feel in the last ten to twenty years. In the pop culture of music, television, and movies the level of crude immorality and violence has increased dramatically. In politics the social agenda of the so-called Christian right has been marginalized and ridiculed. Feeling betrayed by politicians, the public schools, and even many church leaders, many Christians have sought ways to isolate themselves from the evil and degeneration they sense around them. They have sought to create a subculture of their own. The phenomenon of home schooling is one manifestation of that withdrawal. So is the rise of creation science as an antidote to evolution and materialism. This anxious response is a form of circling the wagons tightly for protection and preservation. It is understandable, and elements of it are appropriate. But when it is taken too far, it is dangerous and unbiblical. Just as we must beware of anti-Christian forms of thought that claim to be science, so we must beware of anti-intellectualism and an inappropriate rejection of science parading itself as Christianity. As Christians we must not tie our faith to a pseudoscience of human invention, whether by a fad of secular science or so-called creation science. We must not hobble the evangelistic work of the church by embracing a false science of any kind. Rather we must hold to the teachings of the Bible and evaluate by them the claims of science and of biblical interpretations. We know that ultimately the true interpretation of the Bible and true science must agree. But we must be patient sometimes waiting for that agreement to become clear.

For some defenders of the traditional interpretation of Genesis 1, any departure from their literal reading of the text puts one on an interpretive slippery slope that can turn any text of the Bible into a figure. Some go so far as to ask, If the days of Genesis 1 are a figure, then how can we avoid concluding that Adam or the resurrection of Jesus are figures, not historical realities? This concern is understandable in light of the irresponsible liberal treatments of the Bible that we saw so much of in the twentieth century.

How can we avoid an interpretive slippery slope? First, we need to remember that the slippery slope argument has often been used illegitimately in the history of the church. The Church of Rome in the sixteenth century warned the Reformers that their doctrine of justification was a slippery slope that would lead to an indifference to holiness. The Lutherans in the sixteenth century attacked the Reformed for not accepting their literal and obvious interpretation of the words of Jesus: "This is my body." Many dispensationalists in the twentieth century insisted that we must interpret the Bible literally wherever possible. By literal they meant "without figures" and as a result developed strange views of prophecy. Today those called open theists, who believe that God changes his mind and actions in reaction to human history, claim also to be literal in their interpretation of some biblical passages. We must remember that the excesses of some kinds of literalism are as wrong and dangerous for the church as excesses of figurative readings of the Bible. The church always faces slippery slopes in many directions.

Second, the only way to avoid the slippery slope is the obvious one: we must return over and over again to the careful study of the text of the Bible. We must look at the text and the context to understand any passage. We must compare any text with the teaching of the Bible as a whole. We must follow sound and proven methods of biblical interpretation.[10] When we study the Bible in this way, we will be safe. Those methods show clearly that Adam was a real, historical person, the father of the whole human race. Those methods show that Jesus arose bodily from the grave. Those methods also show that the days of creation are figurative descriptions of the actions of God.

Conclusion

No doubt the approach to Genesis 1 taken in this study will not convince everyone that it is correct, but it should demonstrate that it is an exegesis that is responsible to the text and ought to be tolerable in conservative Protestant circles. This covenantal approach rests on the absolute authority and inerrancy of the Bible. It has been developed on the basis of sound and clear principles of biblical interpretation and is the result of careful exegesis of the biblical texts at hand.

It would be wonderful if this study brought new unity on the understanding of Genesis 1. But at the least it should contribute to an atmosphere of more careful study of Genesis 1 and more careful use of strong words in controversy within our conservative community.

The approach taken to Genesis 1 in this study is a careful examination of the words of Scripture. We have focused on the question of the days of creation and what they mean. We want to summarize the conclusions we have reached about the teaching of the Bible on creation in ten statements.

Ten Theses on Creation

1. Nothing is impossible for God.

    No kind of work is beyond his power, including creating instantaneously or in six twenty-four-hour days if he had chosen to do so.

2. The God of the Bible alone created the heavens and the earth.

    No other god or force caused creation.

3. God created out of nothing.

    God's work of creation was not just the shaping of preexistent materials.

4. Genesis 1 and 2 are true, historical accounts of creation.

    Genesis 1 and 2 are not myth and do not contradict each other.

5. Scripture alone authoritatively interprets the biblical account of creation.

    The claims of modern science cannot determine the interpretation of the Bible.

6. God created the earth for man, his image bearer.

    Other creatures are not of equal value with man in God's sight.

7. God created man immediately from the dust of the earth.

    Man did not evolve from lower animals.

8. Genesis 1 presents God's days of creation as a pattern for man with six days for work and one day for rest.

    The days of Genesis 1 are not primarily about how God created.

9. The Sabbath is a creation ordinance for man.

    Jesus did not abolish the Sabbath but fulfilled and transformed it into the Lord's day.

10. Christians must believe what God has revealed about his work of creation.

    Christians must be careful about imposing the conclusions of their study of creation on other Christians.

Appendix 1

CALVIN ON CREATION
FROM HIS COMMENTARY ON GENESIS 1

An examination of John Calvin's interpretation of Genesis 1 can help us become clear about some of the proper exegetical principles that can guide us today. Calvin was not only one of the best exegetes in the history of the church but also approached the text long before the current controversies about its meaning. He cannot be accused of accommodating to modern science, especially since he concluded from his study that the days of Genesis 1 were ordinary days. We may disagree with some of Calvin's conclusions, but his principles of interpretation are the ones that should guide faithful exegesis. Calvin's approach to the text is basically covenantal.

Calvin does conclude in his study that Genesis 1 is simple chronology and does see the days of creation as ordinary days. He writes forcefully especially against the opinion of Augustine that God created everything in a moment and then described the creation in terms of six days to instruct us:

Here the error of those is manifestly refuted, who maintain that the world was made in a moment. For it is too violent a cavil to contend that Moses distributes the work that God perfected at once into six days, for the mere purpose of conveying instruction. Let us rather conclude that God himself took the space of six days, for the purpose of accommodating his works to the capacity of men. We slightingly pass over the infinite glory of God, which here shines forth; whence arises this but from our excessive dullness in considering his greatness? In the meantime, the vanity of our minds carries us away elsewhere. For the correction of this fault, God applied the most suitable remedy when he distributed the creation of the world into successive portions, that he might fix our attention, and compel us, as if he had laid his hand upon us, to pause and to reflect.[1]

Calvin rejects the idea that the days of Genesis 1 are presented for the "mere purpose" of instructing us. He teaches that the days correspond to reality. But notice his method of interpretation. He recognizes that God chose to create in six days to "accommodate his works" to our "capacity." Here two critical points are made about interpreting the Bible and understanding God. Our capacity as humans to understand is limited. We are finite whereas God is infinite. We are time-bound whereas God is eternal. We live in a physical world whereas God is purely spiritual. The result of our limited capacity is that God must accommodate himself to us when he reveals himself. We cannot see him as he is in himself—remember God telling Moses that he could not see God's glory directly and live! Rather he reveals himself through words that we can understand in relation to human experience and knowledge. Again Calvin writes, "Just as we have before observed, that the creation of the world was distributed over six days, for our sake, to the end that our minds might the more easily be retained in the meditation of God's works."[2]

Calvin uses this principle of accommodation to our capacity in reflecting on God's declaration that what he had created was good. "Here God is introduced by Moses as surveying his work, that he might take pleasure in it. But he does it for our sake, to teach us that God has made nothing without a certain reason and design. And we ought not so to understand the words of Moses as if God did not know that his work was good, till he finished it."[3] God does not need to step back from his creative act, evaluate it, and then reach the conclusion that it was good. God reveals himself as acting in the way a man would act in those circumstances to communicate the pleasure and approval he has for his creation. Similarly Calvin writes, "Moses declares that God approved of everything which he had made. In speaking of God as *seeing,* he does it after the manner of men; for the Lord designed this his judgment to be as a rule and example to us; that no one should dare to think or speak otherwise of his works."[4] The meaning of the text is clear, but the words of the revelation are accommodated to our capacity. As Calvin puts it at another place, "For as it became a theologian, he [Moses] had respect to *us,* rather than to the *stars.*"[5]

Although Calvin does not use the word *covenantal* to describe his approach, the word is an appropriate description. He stresses over and over that the text is given for us. It is not "mere" instruction, but it does teach us about our relation to God. He sees the meaning of the six days as God forcing us to pause and reflect point by point, day by day on the wonders and glories of our God and his creation. We are to learn to ascribe all creation to God and to share in his conclusion that it is good.

Calvin also stresses that God arranged all of creation for humankind. "And hence we infer what was the end for which all things were created; namely, that none of the conveniences and necessaries of life might be wanting to men. In the very order of the creation the paternal solicitude of God for man is conspicuous, because he furnished the world with all things needful, and even with an immense profusion of wealth, before he formed man."[6] Calvin uses this same covenantal approach in interpreting the seventh day. He concludes that God made the seventh day holy for man and notes, "God therefore sanctifies the seventh day, when he renders it illustrious, that by a special law it may be distinguished from the rest. Whence it also appears, that God always had respect to the welfare of men."[7]

The covenantal approach helps Calvin to see clearly that the Bible is not a textbook on science. The Bible is covenantal revelation written for the ordinary believer, not for the scientist: "The history of the creation . . . is the book of the unlearned."[8] "Moses wrote in a popular style things which, without instruction, all ordinary persons, endued with common sense, are able to understand."[9]

Calvin recognizes a useful role for the work of scientists, but it is quite distinct from the character and purpose of biblical revelation: "But astronomers investigate with great labour whatever the sagacity of the human mind can comprehend. Nevertheless, this study is not to be reprobated, nor this science to be condemned, because some frantic persons are wont boldly to reject whatever is unknown to them. For astronomy is not only pleasant, but also very useful to be known: it cannot be denied that this art unfolds the admirable wisdom of God."[10]

While the Bible and science are distinct for Calvin, he affirms clearly the superior authority of the Bible. If the two seem to conflict, he asserts authority of the Bible, especially regarding creation since creation is such a unique work of God. For example on the creation of the birds, he writes:

It seems, however, but little consonant with reason, that he declares birds to have proceeded from the waters; and, therefore, this is seized upon by captious men as an occasion of calumny. But although there should appear no other reason but that it so pleased God, would it not be becoming in us to acquiesce in his judgment? . . . And, truly, the Lord, although he is the Author of nature, yet by no means has followed nature as his guide in the creation of the world, but has rather chosen to put forth such demonstrations of his power as should constrain us to wonder.[11]

Calvin sees a culmination of creation in the blessing of the seventh day. See how he celebrates the importance and centrality of that day in the economy of creation:

> Wherefore, that benediction is nothing else than a solemn consecration, by which God claims for himself the meditations and employments of men on the seventh day. This is, indeed, the proper business of the whole life, in which men should daily exercise themselves, to consider the infinite goodness, justice, power, and wisdom of God, in this magnificent theatre of heaven and earth. But, lest men should prove less sedulously attentive to it than they ought, every seventh day has been especially selected for the purpose of supplying what was wanting in daily meditation. First, therefore, God rested; then he blessed this rest, that in all ages it might be held sacred among men: or he dedicated every seventh day to rest, that his own example might be a perpetual rule. The design of the institution must be always kept in memory: for God did not command men simply to keep holiday every seventh day, as if he delighted in their indolence; but rather that they, being released from all other business, might the more readily apply their minds to the Creator of the world. Lastly, that is a sacred rest which withdraws men from the impediments of the world, that it may dedicate them entirely to God.[12]

Seeing the importance of the seventh day and the example that God gave people in it, Calvin then asks how we should understand the idea of God resting.

> The question may not improperly be put, what kind of rest this was. For it is certain that inasmuch as God sustains the world by his power, governs it by his providence, cherishes, and even propagates all creatures, he is constantly at work. Therefore that saying of Christ is true, that the Father and he himself had worked from the beginning hitherto [John 5:17], because, if God should but withdraw his hand a little, all things would immediately perish and dissolve into nothing, as is declared in Psalm civ. 29.[13]

This question is so important for Calvin for two reasons. First, he wants to remove any hint of apparent contradiction between Moses, who said that God rested on the Sabbath, and Jesus, who said he did not. Second, Calvin wants to clarify a vital theological point for him: all creation is always purely contingent, that is, it has not life in itself but exists only as God actively works to maintain its existence. Calvin finds the solution to the question in a traditional distinction: "The solution of the difficulty is well known, that God ceased from all his work, when he desisted from the creation of new kinds of things."[14] In other words, on the seventh day God rested from the works of creation, although he continued the works of providence.

We should learn one final point from Calvin, this one negative. We must beware of reading our theological convictions into the text. Let me offer an example where Calvin may have done so. Calvin addresses the question as to how there could be light created on the first day when the sun as the light giver was not created until the fourth day. Calvin explains the reason for God's acting in this way: "Therefore the Lord, by the very order of the creation, bears witness that he holds in his hand the light, which he is able to impart to us without the sun and moon."[15] He sees another example of this in the growth of vegetation before the creation of the sun: "We now see, indeed, that the earth is quickened by the sun to cause it to bring forth its fruits; nor was God ignorant of this law of nature, which he has since ordained: but in order that we might learn to refer all things to him, he did not then make use of the sun or moon."[16] Both of these cases illustrate the important theological truth that he expresses: "We acknowledge, it is true, in words, that the First Cause is self-sufficient, and that intermediate and secondary causes have only what they borrow from this First Cause; but, in reality, we picture God to ourselves as poor or imperfect, unless he is assisted by second causes."[17]

This theological principle is important to Calvin not only for understanding the pure contingency of all creation but also for his doctrine of the sacraments. Calvin insists that in appointing the sacraments as a means of grace, God does not give them power in themselves. They always depend on the action of God to be effective. Here too the dependence of secondary causes on the First Cause is asserted. This point is a key element in the radical stress of Calvin on the sovereignty of God.

Calvin is correct on the theological point he is making. Secondary causes are always dependent on the First Cause for their efficacy. And God is never dependent on secondary causes to accomplish his purposes. But the correctness of the point does not mean that it is being taught by God in Genesis 1:3 or Genesis 1:11. It may be, or it may not. We must beware of reading too much into a text. The proper theological lessons can be learned from a text only after its meaning is properly determined.

We can summarize the principles of interpretation that we have derived from Calvin's study of Genesis 1:

(1) look for the reality of the history of creation;
(2) recognize that in the text God is accommodating himself to our capacity;
(3) look for the covenantal message that God has for us, his people;
(4) recognize that the Bible and science are different;
(5) assert the authority of the Bible over science;
(6) recognize that the institution of the Sabbath is a key part of understanding the character and meaning of creation;
(7) beware of reading our theological principles, even good ones, into texts where they are not really taught.

We need to keep these principles clearly in mind as we seek to understand the teaching of Genesis 1. The interpretation of Genesis 1 presented in our study does not reach the same conclusion as Calvin on the days of creation but uses precisely his method of literal, historical-grammatical interpretation.

2 Esdras 6:35–59

Most scholars think that the section of the Second Book of Esdras quoted below was written in the first century A.D. The words cited below are presented as a prayer of Ezra:

"Now after this I wept again and fasted seven days as before, in order to complete the three weeks as I had been told. And on the eighth night my heart was troubled within me again, and I began to speak in the presence of the Most High. For my spirit was greatly aroused, and my soul was in distress.

I said, "O Lord, thou didst speak at the beginning of creation, and didst say on the first day, 'Let heaven and earth be made,' and thy word accomplished the work. And then the Spirit was hovering, and darkness and silence embraced everything; the sound of man's voice was not yet there. Then thou didst command that a ray of light be brought forth from thy treasuries, so that thy works might then appear.

"Again, on the second day, thou didst create the spirit of the firmament, and didst command him to divide and separate the waters, that one part might move upward and the other part remain beneath.

"On the third day thou didst command the waters to be gathered together in the seventh part of the earth; six parts thou didst dry up and keep so that some of them might be planted and cultivated and be of service before thee. For thy word went forth, and at once the work was done. For immediately fruit came forth in endless abundance and of varied appeal to the taste; and flowers of inimitable color; and odors of inexpressible fragrance. These were made on the third day.

"On the fourth day thou didst command the brightness of the sun, the light of the moon, and the arrangement of the stars to come into being; and thou didst command them to serve man, who was about to be formed.

"On the fifth day thou didst command the seventh part, where the water had been gathered together, to bring forth living creatures, birds and fishes; and so it was done. The dumb and lifeless water produced living creatures, as it was commanded, that therefore the nations might declare thy wondrous works.

"Then thou didst keep in existence two living creatures; the name of one thou didst call Behemoth and the name of the other Leviathan. And thou didst separate one from the other, for the seventh part where the water had been gathered together could not hold them both. And thou didst give Behemoth one of the parts which had been dried up on the third day, to live in it, where there are a thousand mountains; but to Leviathan thou didst give the seventh part, the watery part; and thou hast kept them to be eaten by whom thou wilt, and when thou wilt.

"On the sixth day thou didst command the earth to bring forth before thee cattle, beasts, and creeping things; and over these thou didst place Adam, as ruler over all the works which thou hadst made; and from him we have all come, the people whom thou hast chosen.

"All this I have spoken before thee, O Lord, because thou hast said that it was for us that thou didst create this world. As for the other nations which have descended from Adam, thou hast said that they are nothing, and that they are like spittle, and thou hast compared their abundance to a drop from a bucket. And now, O Lord, behold, these nations, which are reputed as nothing, domineer over us and devour us. But we thy people, whom thou hast called thy firstborn, only begotten, zealous for thee, and most dear, have been given into their hands. If the world has indeed been created for us, why do we not possess our world as an inheritance? How long will this be so?"[1]

THE REFORMED CONFESSIONS ON CREATION

M y reading of the following Reformed confessions leads me to make these observations:

1. The confessions make references to matters related to Genesis 1 and 2 in discussions of creation, original sin, or the fourth commandment.
2. All of the confessions make clear that God created the heavens and the earth out of nothing.
3. All of the confessions make clear their conviction that Adam was the first human being and the father of the whole human race.
4. Only the Genevan Catechism and the Westminster Standards refer to six days of creation (other than in quoting the fourth commandment.) The Genevan Catechism Q. 177 assumes and affirms that creation occurred in six days. That point is made to underscore that God's rest is an example to us to help us be conformed to his image. In the

Westminster Standards the confession of creation includes the phrase "in the space of six days" (Confession 4.1; Larger Catechism 15; Shorter Catechism 9).

THE FIRST HELVETIC CONFESSION (1536)

Article 8. Original Sin

And this plague, which they call original, so pervades all humanity that a child of wrath and enemy of God could be cured by no other work than by a divine one through Christ.

THE CATECHISM OF THE CHURCH OF GENEVA (1545)

Q. 25.   Why do you add: Maker of heaven and earth?

A.   Because he manifested himself to us through his works, and in them he is to be sought by us (Ps. 104; Rom. 1:20). For our mind is incapable of entertaining his essence. Therefore there is the world itself as a kind of mirror, in which we may observe him, in so far as it concerns us to know him.

Q. 167.   Does he order us to labour six days, in order that we may rest on the seventh?

A.   Not exactly: but he permits six days for men's labours, and excludes the seventh, that it may be devoted to rest.

Q. 176.   Why, then, is the seventh rather than any other day prescribed?

A.   This number denotes perfection in Scripture. Therefore it is suitable to indicate perpetuity. At the same time, it suggests that this spiritual rest only begins in this life, and does not reach perfection until we depart this world.

Q. 177.   But what is the meaning of the Lord exhorting us by his own example to rest?

A.   When he finished the creation of the world in six days, he dedicated the seventh to the contemplation of his works. To incite us more strongly to this, he sets before us his own example. For nothing is more to be desired than that we be formed in his image.

THE FRENCH CONFESSION OF FAITH (1559)

Article 7. We believe that God, in three co-working persons, by his power, wisdom, and incomprehensible goodness, created all things, not only the heavens and the earth and all that in them is, but also invisible spirits. . . .

Article 10. We believe that all the posterity of Adam is in bondage to original sin, which is an hereditary evil, and not an imitation merely, as was declared by the Pelagians, whom we detest in their errors. And we consider that it is not necessary to inquire how sin was conveyed from one man to another, for what God had given Adam was not for him alone, but for all his posterity; and thus in his person

113

we have been deprived of all good things, and have fallen with him into a state of sin and misery.

THE FIRST SCOTS CONFESSION (1560)

Article 2. Of the Creation of Man

We confess and acknowledge this our God to have created man, to wit, our first father Adam, to his own image and similitude, to whom he gave wisdom, lordship, justice, free-will, and clear knowledge of himself, so that in the whole nature of man there could be no imperfection. From which honor and perfection, man and woman did both fall. . . .

Article 3. Of Original Sin

By which transgression, commonly called Original sin, was the image of God utterly defaced in man, and he and his posterity of nature become enemies of God, slaves to Satan, and servants unto sin. . . .

THE BELGIC CONFESSION (1561)

Article 2. By What Means God Is Made Known unto Us

We know Him by two means: First, by the creation, preservation, and government of the universe; which is before our eyes as a most elegant book, wherein all creatures, great and small, are as so many characters leading us to "see clearly the invisible things of God," even "his ever-lasting power and divinity. . . ."

Article 12. The Creation of All Things, Especially the Angels

We believe that the Father by the Word, that is, by His Son, has created out of nothing the heaven, the earth, and all creatures, when it seemed good unto Him, giving unto every creature its being, shape, form, and several offices to serve its Creator; that He also still upholds and governs them by His eternal providence and infinite power for the service of mankind, to the end that man may serve his God. . . ."

Article 14. The Creation and Fall of Man, and His Incapacity to Perform What Is Truly Good

We believe that God created man out of the dust of the earth, and made and formed him after His own image and likeness, good, righteous, and holy, capable in all things to will agreeable to the will of God. . . .

Article 15. Original Sin

We believe that through the disobedience of Adam original sin is extended to all mankind; which is a corruption of the whole nature and a hereditary disease, wherewith even infants in their mother's womb are infected. . . .

Article 16. Eternal Election

We believe that, all the posterity of Adam being thus fallen into perdition and ruin by the sin of our first parents,

God then did manifest Himself such as He is; that is to say, merciful and just. . . .

HEIDELBERG CATECHISM (1563)

Q. 6.   Did God, then, create man so wicked and perverse?

A.   By no means; but God created man good, and after His own image; that is, in true righteousness and holiness, that he might rightly know God his Creator, heartily love Him, and live with Him in eternal blessedness to praise and glorify Him.

Q. 7.   Whence, then, comes this depraved nature of man?

A.   From the fall and disobedience of our first parents, Adam and Eve, in Paradise, whereby our nature became so corrupt that we all are conceived and born in sin.

Q. 26.   What do you believe when you say: I believe in God the Father, Almighty, Maker of heaven and earth?

A.   That the eternal Father of our Lord Jesus Christ, who of nothing made heaven and earth with all that is in them, who likewise upholds and governs the same by His eternal counsel and providence, is for the sake of Christ His Son my God and my Father. . . .

Q. 28.   What does it profit us to know that God has created, and by His providence still upholds, all things?

A.   That we may be patient in adversity, thankful in prosperity, and with a view to the future may have good confidence in our faithful God and Father that no creature shall separate us from His love, since all creatures are so in His hand that without His will they cannot so much as move.

Q. 103. What does God require of us in the fourth commandment?

A.   First, that the ministry of the gospel and the schools be maintained; and that I, especially on the Sabbath, that is, the day of rest, diligently attend the church of God, to learn God's Word, to use the sacraments, to call publicly upon the Lord, and to give Christian alms. Second, that all the days of my life I rest from my evil works, let the Lord work in me by His Holy Spirit, and thus begin in this life the eternal Sabbath.

THE THIRTY-NINE ARTICLES OF THE CHURCH OF ENGLAND (1563)

Article 9. Of Original or Birth-Sin

Original sin standeth not in the following of Adam (as the Pelagians vainly talk); but it is the fault and corruption of the Nature of every man, that naturally is engendered of the offspring of Adam; whereby man is very far gone from original righteousness, and is of his own nature inclined to evil, so that the flesh lusteth always contrary to the spirit; and therefore in every person born into this world, it deserveth God's wrath and damnation. . . .

THE SECOND HELVETIC CONFESSION (1566)

Article 7. Of the Creation of all Things; Angels, the Devil, and Man

1. This good and almighty God created all things, both visible and invisible, by His eternal Word, and preserves the same also by His eternal Spirit: as David witnesses, saying, "By the word of the Lord were the heavens made; and all the host of them by the breath of His mouth" (Ps. 33:6); and, as the Scripture says, "And God saw every thing that He had made, and behold, it was very good" (Gen. 1:31)[1], and made for the use and profit of man.

2. Now, we say, that all those things do proceed from one beginning: and therefore we detest the Manichees and the Marcionites, who did wickedly imagine two substances and natures, the one of good and the other of evil; and also two beginnings and two gods, one contrary to the other—a good and an evil.

3. Among all creatures, the angels and men are the most excellent. Touching angels, the Holy Scripture says, "who maketh His angels spirits, His ministers a flaming fire" (Ps. 104:4); also, "Are they not all ministering spirits, sent forth to minister for them who shall be heirs of salvation?" (Heb. 1:14).

4. And the Lord Jesus Himself testifies of the devil, saying, "He was a murderer from the beginning, and abode

not in the truth, because there is no truth in him. When he speaketh a lie, he speaketh of his own: for he is a liar, and the father of it" (John 8:44).

5. We, teach, therefore, that some angels persisted in obedience, and were appointed unto the faithful service of God and men; and that others fell of their own accord, and ran headlong into destruction, and so became enemies to all good, and to all the faithful, etc.

6. Now, touching man, the Spirit says that in the beginning he was created according to the image and likeness of God (Gen. 1:27); that God placed him in Paradise, and made all things subject unto him; which David doth most nobly set forth in the 8th Psalm. Moreover, God gave unto him a wife, and blessed them.

7. We say, also that man doth consist of two, and those diverse substances in one person; of a soul immortal (as that which being separated from his body doth neither sleep nor die), and a body mortal, which, notwithstanding, at the last judgment shall be raised again from the dead, that from henceforth the whole man may continue forever in life or in death.

8. We condemn all those who mock at, or by subtle disputations call into doubt, the immortality of the soul, or say that the soul sleeps or that it is a part of God. To be short, we condemn all opinions of all men whatsoever who think otherwise of the creation of angels, devils, and men than is delivered unto us by the Scriptures in the Apostolic Church of Christ.

Article 8. Of Man's Fall; Sin, and the Cause of Sin

1. Man was from the beginning created of God after the image of God, in righteousness and true holiness, good

and upright; but by the instigation of the serpent and his own fault, falling from the goodness and uprightness, he became subject to sin, death, and divers calamities; and such a one as he became by his fall, such are all his offspring, even subject to sin, death, and sundry calamities.

2. And we take sin to be that natural corruption of man, derived or spread from our first parents unto us all, through which we, being drowned in evil concupiscence, and clean turned away from God, but prone to all evil, full of all wickedness, distrust, contempt, and hatred of God, can do no good of ourselves—no, not so much as think any (Matt. 12:34–35).

5. We therefore acknowledge that original sin is in all men; we acknowledge that all other sins which spring therefrom are both called and are indeed sins, by what name soever they may be termed, whether mortal or venial, or also that which is called sin against the Holy Spirit, which is never forgiven.

WESTMINSTER CONFESSION OF FAITH (1647)

Chapter I, Of the Holy Scripture

1. Although the light of nature, and the works of creation and providence do so far manifest the goodness, wisdom, and power of God, as to leave men inexcusable; yet are they not sufficient to give the knowledge of God, and of his will, which is necessary unto salvation. . . .

Chapter IV, Of Creation

1. It pleased God the Father, Son, and Holy Ghost, for the manifestation of the glory of his eternal power, wisdom, and goodness, in the beginning, to create, or make of nothing, the world, and all things therein whether visible or invisible, in the space of six days; and all very good.

Chapter VI, Of the Fall of Man, of Sin, and of the Punishment Thereof

1. Our first parents, being seduced by the subtelty and temptation of Satan, sinned, in eating the forbidden fruit. . . .

Chapter VII, Of God's Covenant with Man

2. The first covenant made with man was a covenant of works, wherein life was promised to Adam; and in him to his posterity, upon condition of perfect and personal obedience.

Chapter XXI, Of Religious Worship, and the Sabbath Day

1. The light of nature showeth that there is a God, who hath lordship and sovereignty over all, is good, and doth good unto all, and is therefore to be feared, loved, praised, called upon, trusted in, and served, with all the heart, and with all the soul, and with all the might. But the acceptable way of worshipping the true God is instituted by himself, and so limited by his own revealed will, that he may not be worshiped according to the imaginations and devices of men, or the suggestions of Satan, under any visible rep-

resentation, or any other way not prescribed in the Holy Scripture.

7. As it is the law of nature, that, in general, a due proportion of time be set apart for the worship of God; so, in his Word, by a positive, moral, and perpetual commandment binding all men in all ages, he hath particularly appointed one day in seven, for a Sabbath, to be kept holy unto him. . . .

THE LARGER CATECHISM (1647)

Q. 2.   How doth it appear that there is a God?

A.   The very light of nature in man, and the works of God, declare plainly that there is a God; . . .

Q. 15.   What is the work of creation?

A.   The work of creation is that wherein God did in the beginning, by the word of his power, make of nothing the world, and all things therein, for himself, within the space of six days, and all very good.

Q. 21.   Did man continue in that estate wherein God at first created him?

A.   Our first parents being left to the freedom of their own will, through the temptation of Satan, transgressed. . . .

Q. 22.   Did all mankind fall in that first transgression?

A.   The covenant being made with Adam as a public person, not for himself only, but for his posterity, all mankind descending from him by ordinary generation, sinned in him, and fell with him in that first transgression.

Q. 26. How is original sin conveyed from our first parents unto their posterity?

A. Original sin is conveyed from our first parents unto their posterity by natural generation, so as all that proceed from them in that way are conceived and born in sin.

Q. 116. What is required in the fourth commandment?

A. The fourth commandment requireth of all men the sanctifying or keeping holy to God such set times as he hath appointed in his word, expressly one whole day in seven. . . .

Q. 120. What are the reasons annexed to the fourth commandment, the more to enforce it?

A. The reasons annexed to the fourth commandment, the more to enforce it, are taken from the equity of it, God allowing us six days of seven for our own affairs, and reserving but one for himself, in these words, *Six days shalt thou* labor, and do all thy work: from God's challenging a special propriety in that day, *The seventh day is the Sabbath of the Lord thy God:* from the example of God, *who in six days made heaven and earth, the sea, and all that in them is, and rested the seventh day.* . . .

THE SHORTER CATECHISM (1647)

Q. 9.   What is the work of creation?

A.   The work of creation is, God's making all things of nothing, by the word of his power, in the space of six days, and all very good.

Q. 16.   Did all mankind fall in Adam's first transgression?

A.   The covenant being made with Adam, not only for himself, but for his posterity; all mankind, descending from him by ordinary generation, sinned in him, and fell with him, in his first transgression.

Q. 58.   What is required in the fourth commandment?

A.   The fourth commandment requireth the keeping holy to God such set times as he hath appointed in his Word; expressly one whole day in seven, to be a holy Sabbath to himself.

Q. 62.   What are the reasons annexed to the fourth commandment?

A.   The reasons annexed to the fourth commandment are, God's allowing us six days of the week for our own employments, his challenging a special propriety in the seventh, his own example, and his blessing the Sabbath day.

"Six Days" in the Westminster Standards

Theologians from the eighteenth century to the present have reflected on the meaning of "in the space of six days" in the Westminster Standards. Below are excerpts from the writings of Thomas Ridgeley (1667–1734), English Independent pastor; Thomas Boston (1676–1732), Church of Scotland minister; Ashbel Green (1762–1848), pastor in the Presbyterian Church in Pennsylvania; Robert Shaw (1795–1863), Scottish pastor in the Original Succession Church; A. A. Hodge (1823–1886), Presbyterian minister and theologian at Princeton Theological Seminary; and John Macpherson (1847–1902), pastor in the Free Church of Scotland. From the twentieth century are James Harper, professor of theology at Theological Seminary in Xenia, Ohio; G. I. Williamson, pastor in the Orthodox Presbyterian Church; Gordon Clark, professor and Calvinist philosopher; David W. Hall, senior fellow at The Kuyper Institute and pastor in the Presbyterian Church in America; and William S. Barker, church history professor at Westminster Theological Seminary and president of Covenant Theological Seminary.

THOMAS RIDGELEY (1731)

We are now to consider the space of time, in which God created all things, namely, in six days. This could not have been determined by the light of nature, and therefore must be concluded to be a doctrine of pure revelation. . . . Here we cannot but take notice of the opinion of some who suppose that the world was created in an instant. They think, that this is more agreeable to the idea of creation, and more plainly distinguishes it from the natural production of things, which are brought to perfection by degrees, and not in a moment, as they suppose this work was. This opinion has been advanced by some ancient writers. And as it seems directly to contradict that account which is given by Moses, they suppose that the distribution of the work of creation into six days, is designed only to lead us into the knowledge of the distinct parts of the work, whereby they may be better conceived of, as though they had been made in the order described one after another. But this is to make the scripture speak what men please to have it, without any regard to the genuine sense and import of its words. . . .

There is, therefore, another account given of this matter, by some divines of very considerable worth and judgment, which, as they apprehend, concedes as much as needs to be demanded in favour of the instantaneous production of things, as most agreeable to the idea of creation, and yet does not militate against the sense of the account given in Gen. i., and that is, that the distinct parts of the creation were each produced in a moment. . . . The main objection brought against their opinion who plead for an instantaneous production of things in each day, is, that for God to bring the work of each day to perfection in a moment, and afterwards not to begin the work of the next day till the respective day began, infers God's resting each day from his work; while he is not said to rest till the whole creation was brought to perfection. But I cannot see this to be a just consequence, or sufficient to overthrow the opinion. God's resting from his work when the whole was finished, means principally his not producing any new species of creatures, and not merely his ceasing to produce what he had made.[1]

THOMAS BOSTON (1773)

Our next business is to shew in what space of time the world was created. It was not done in a moment, but in the space of six days, as is clear from the narrative of Moses. It was as easy for God to have done it in one moment as in six days. But this method he took, that we might have that wisdom, goodness, and power that appeared in the work, distinctly before our eyes, and be stirred up to a particular and distinct consideration of these works, for commemoration of which a seventh day is appointed a sabbath of rest. . . .

But although God did not make all things in one moment, yet we are to believe, that every particular work was done in a moment, seeing it was done by a word, or an act of the divine will, Psal. xxxiii. 9. forecited.

No sooner was the divine will intimated, than the thing willed instantly took place.[2]

ASHBEL GREEN, 1841

It was *in the space of six days* that God created all things. No doubt it had been equally easy with God to have made all things in an instant of time. But as it helps our conceptions of the work of creation, now that it is formed, to think of its gradual production, so there were other wise purposes to be answered by it. An example of alternate labour and rest was hereby set, which was intended to be of use in every successive age. And the proper portion of time, to be set apart for the immediate worship of God, and the cultivation of a holy and heavenly temper, was in this manner fixed by the divine appointment. . . .

But I must not fail to warn you against giving in to any of the fanciful theories—I think them impious as well as fanciful—which you may perhaps meet with in reading, and which all go to represent the Mosaic account of the creation *as not strictly and historically true.* One of these writers will have this account to be a mere fable; another, not a fable exactly, but a *mythos,* or scheme, or story of explanation; another, an allegory, and I know not what beside. Alas! Who made these men the correctors of Moses, the great prophet of God? He delivers what he says as unquestionable facts. As such they were no doubt revealed to him by God, and as such we are bound to receive them.[3]

ROBERT SHAW (1845)

That the world, and all things therein, were created "in the space of six days." This, also is the express language of Scripture: "For in six days the Lord made heaven and earth, the sea, and all that in them is." —Ex. xx.11. The modern discoveries of geologists have led them to assign an earlier origin to the materials of which our globe is composed than the period of the six days, commonly known by the name of the Mosaic creation; and various theories have been adopted in order to reconcile the geological and Mosaic records. Some have held that all the changes which have taken place in the materials of the earth occurred either during the six days of the Mosaic creation, or since that period; but, it is urged, that the facts which geology establishes prove this view to be utterly untenable. Others have held that a day of creation was not a natural day, composed of twenty-four hours, but a period of an indefinite length. To this it has been objected, that the sacred historian, as if to guard against such a latitude of interpretation, distinctly and pointedly declares of all the days, that each of them had its "evening and morning,"—thus, it should seem, expressly excluding any interpretation which does not imply a natural day. Others hold that the materials of our globe were in existence, and under the active operation of creative powers, for an indefinite period before the creation of man; and that the inspired record, while it gives us no information respecting the pre-existing condition of the earth, leaves ample room for a belief that it did pre-exist, if from any other source traces of this should be

129

discovered by human research. The first verse of the first chapter of Genesis, in their opinion, merely asserts that the matter of which the universe is composed was produced out of nothing by the power of the Almighty, but leaves the time altogether indefinite. The subsequent verses of that chapter give an account of the successive process by which the Eternal, in the space of six days, reduced the pre-existing matter to its present form, and gave being to the plants and animals now in existence. This explanation, which leaves room for a long succession of geological events before the creation of the existing races, seems now to be the generally received mode of reconciling geological discoveries with the Mosaic account of the creation.[4]

A. A. HODGE (1869)

This section, using the precise words of Scripture, Ex. xx. 11, declares that God performed the work of creation, in the sense of formation and adjustment of the universe in its present order, "in the space of six days." Since the Confession was written the science of geology has come into existence, and has brought to light many facts before unknown as to the various conditions through which this world, and probably the stellar universe, have passed previously to the establishment of the present order. These facts remain in their general character unquestionable, and indicate a process of divinely regulated development consuming vast periods of time. In order to adjust the conclusions of that science with the inspired record found in the first chapter of Genesis, some suppose that the first verse relates to the creation of the elements of things at the absolute beginning, and then, after a vast interval, during which the changes discovered by science took place, the second and subsequent verses narrate how God in six successive days reconstructed and prepared the world and its inhabitants for the residence of man. Others have supposed that the days spoken of are not natural days, but cycles of vast duration. No adjustment thus far suggested has been found to remove all difficulty. The facts which are certain are:—(1.) The record in Genesis has been given by divine revelation, and therefore is infallibly true. (2.) The book of revelation and the book of nature are both from God, and will be found, when both are adequately interpreted, to coincide perfectly. (3.) The facts upon which the science of geology is based are as yet very imperfectly collected and much more imperfectly understood. The time has not come yet in which a profitable comparison and adjustment of the two records can be attempted. (4.) The record in Genesis, brief and general as it is, was designed and is admirably adapted to lay the foundation of an intelligent faith in Jehovah as the absolute creator and the immediate former and providential ruler of all things. But it was not designed either to prevent or to take the place of a scientific interpretation of all existing phenomena, and of all traces of the past history of the world which God allows men to discover. Apparent discrepancies in established truths can have their ground only in imperfect knowledge. God requires us both to believe and to learn. He imposes upon us at present the necessity of humility and patience.[5]

JOHN MACPHERSON (1882)

Much unreasonable opposition has been shown against the intention in our Confession of the statement, "in the space of six days." It might be answer enough to those who thus complain, to remark that their complaint must tell equally against the Scriptures, and also that whatever fair explanation can be given of the scriptural account is equally available for that of the Confession. This has been from earliest times a much debated point from the side of science and from the side of theology. . . .

The student of God's Word need not pledge himself to any theory. The statement of the Confession is purely biblical.[6]

JAMES HARPER (1905)

Q. 6. How much time was occupied in these operations?
A. The Scriptures say six days. Gen. 1:31; Ex. 20:11.

Q. 7. Is it necessary to understand by those days six ordinary solar days?
A. It seems not necessary.

Q. 8. Why is it not necessary?
A. a. Because the word "day" is used to denote a measure of time exhausted before the sun was established as an index, or recorder, of its flight. Gen. 1:5, 7, 13.

b. Because the word "day" is used in Scripture with a great latitude of meaning. Gen. 2:4; 1:5; Jn. 8:56; 9:4; 2 Cor. 6:2; Is. 11:10,11; 63:4.

Q. 9. Does not the fact that we are required to rest one natural, or solar, day in seven imply that the seventh day on which God rested was a solar day, and, if so, that the other six days were the same?

A. No. Our work and rest are to be in the same proportion, but not necessarily of the same duration as God's work and rest.

Q. 10. Has God's rest day been even yet completed?

A. No. The formula used at the end of the work of each of the first six days is not repeated in connection with the seventh day. It is not said, "and the evening and the morning were the seventh day." God's seventh day, we may infer, is not yet ended, and, if so, it is much more than a natural, or solar, day.[7]

G. I. WILLIAMSON (1964)

Perhaps the chief point at which it is commonly thought that science "contradicts" Scripture is where the Bible says that the process of forming the original stuff of creation into its finished state took place in six days. . . . Third, there is the assumption that the six days of creation (as recorded in the Bible) present us with a creation which occurred in six twenty-four-hour days. In reply we may observe that long before "modern science" challenged Bible believers, many Bible believers held on biblical grounds that creation did not occur in six twenty-four-hour periods. It was recognized by them that the Hebrew term (*yom*) is not restricted to this sense. (See John 8:56; Isa. 49:8; Hosea 2:15;

Ps. 110:3; and Job 15:23.) Augustine, for example, recognized that one of the "days" of creation effected the conditions necessary for solar time. Other Bible believers have suggested that the six days of creation were six days during which God revealed to Moses the story of creation. No one saw it happen but God. Moses could "see it" only by way of visions. And these visions may have taken six days to unfold. . . . For our part we can see no good reason to doubt that God did create the world in six twenty-four-hour days, with the appearance of age (that is, with maturity) in the things created, and that the fossils were caused by a great catastrophe, probably the flood, which occurred after creation entirely.[8]

GORDON CLARK (1979)

That the Bible is not a book on science is often given as an excuse for its many alleged mistakes. The assumption seems to be that science books do not make mistakes. But over the centuries scientific theories have come and gone. . . . Of course, the Bible is not a science textbook, but when it mentions natural phenomena, it speaks the truth.

Then there is the matter of the six creative days. Does the word *day* necessarily mean twenty-four hours? In English *day* most frequently means about twelve hours. We also say that there were no telephones in George Washington's day. Further, Genesis 2:4 seems to refer to all six days as one day. And again, can we speak of six days of creation when the first chapter of Genesis uses the verb *create* only three times? . . .

The suspicion that the days of creation were not twenty-four-hour days is not a recent attempt to harmonize modern science and the Bible. Perhaps some Christians whose faith has been shaken by naturalistic science have been so motivated. But our opponents, who are so quick to ridicule Bishop Ussher, usually fail to mention that fact that Augustine, the great theologian of the early fifth century, considered the six creative days to be six periods of time—and he was not motivated by nineteenth century science.[9]

DAVID W. HALL (1999)

Below is my updated argument, limited to Westminster divines only (not including the numerous other contemporaries as did the earlier study), and defending how quantitatively and qualitatively compelling the view remains that their original intent was only in favor of understanding normal days for the confessional phrase "in the space of six days."[10]

WILLIAM S. BARKER (2000)

David Hall has misunderstood this statement [of the Westminster Theological Seminary in Philadelphia] to mean that some Westminster Divines actually taught or entertained a view of long-age days or of a literary framework, but all that the statement is claiming is that the language "in the space of six days" does not exclude such possibilities, as further exegetical work might be pursued as to the nature of the six days of creation in Genesis 1. The issue is not whether any of the Westminster Divines held a view of long ages or of a literary framework, as Hall repeatedly claims, but whether the confessional language requires a view of six twenty-four-hour days and nothing else. . . . The Westminster Divines were, of course, aware of Augustine's writings on the days of creation. . . . The Westminster Divines would have good reason, therefore, to stress the duration of time in the days of creation.[11]

Notes

Introduction

1. By Genesis 1 in this study I mean Gen. 1:1–2:3, the introductory material at the beginning of the Book of Genesis.

2. The only way to determine the meaning of the days of Genesis 1 is by comparing Scripture with Scripture. We must avoid treating the days of Genesis 1 as brute facts standing beyond any need for interpretation.

3. Augustine, *The City of God,* book 11, chapter 7.

4. A fuller discussion of aspects of the framework interpretation is presented under day five. Readers interested in fuller presentations of most of these views should consult *The Genesis Debate,* ed. David G. Hagopian (Mission Viejo, Calif.: Crux Press, 2001).

5. For a full discussion of Calvin's principles of analysis, see appendix 1.

6. In the NIV these words are rendered, "This is the account of," which does not make clear the historical progress through the generations that Moses is laying out.

Chapter 1: The First Three Days of Creation

1. The verb *hover* used here is also used of birds. See Deut. 32:11 and Isa. 31:5.

2. These terms are used separately or together in 1 Sam. 12:21; Job 26:7; Ps. 107:40; Isa. 23:1; 24:10; 27:10; 32:14; 34:11; 45:18; and Jer. 4:23.

3. For these and other numerical features of Genesis 1, see Henri Blocher, *In the Beginning* (Downers Grove, Ill.: InterVarsity Press, 1984), 33.

Chapter 2: The Final Four Days of Creation

1. Gordon Wenham, *Genesis 1–15,* Word Biblical Commentary (Waco, Tex.: Word, 1987), 21–22. The analysis of the structure presented in this study is somewhat different from Wenham's.

2. Nils Wilhelm Lund, *Chiasmus in the New Testament* (Chapel Hill, N.C.: University of North Carolina Press, 1942), 31.

3. Ibid., 32.

4. My colleague Dr. Steven Baugh pointed out this example to me.

5. John Calvin, *Commentaries on the Four Last Books of Moses,* 4 vols. (Grand Rapids, Mich.: Baker, 1979), 3:295.

6. Ibid., 3:358. For the same point, see O. T. Allis, *The Old Testament: Its Claims and Its Critics* (Nutley, N.J.: P&R, 1972), 97–110.

7. The number seven is particularly plentiful as a symbol in the Book of Revelation: not only seven churches and seven spirits, but also seven lampstands, stars, angels, seals, horns, eyes, trumpets, thunders, heads, crowns, last plagues, golden bowls, hills, and kings.

8. For an excellent recent presentation of such an interpretation, see G. K. Beale, *The Book of Revelation: A Commentary on the Greek Text* (Grand Rapids, Mich.: Eerdmans, 1999).

9. We cannot discuss the interpretation of Matthew fully here. Some suggestions that commentators have made include John Calvin, who suggested that Matthew was providing an aid to memory and a survey of the fortunes of the tribe of Judah (John Calvin, *Calvin's Commentaries, A Harmony of the Gospels,* 3 vols. [Grand Rapids, Mich.: Eerdmans, 1975], 1:55, 58). F. W. Grosheide summarized two options: Matthew used fourteen because the number of God is three, the number of man is four, and the number is doubled for the God-man, Jesus; the number of David's name in Hebrew is fourteen, so each set of generations are related to David (F. W. Grosheide, *Het Heilig Evangelie volgens Mattheus* [Kampen: Kok, 1954], 21. Lee Irons, with Meredith Kline, suggests, "The author purposely wanted to stress this numerical system, primarily because of its sabbatical symbolism ($3 \times 14 = 6 \times 7$); the generation of the Messiah represents the seventh seven, thereby showing that it is He who inaugurates the ultimate Sabbath rest for the people of God" in Lee Irons, with Meredith Kline, "The Framework View," in *The Genesis Debate,* ed. David G. Hagopian (Mission Viejo, Calif.: Crux Press, 2001), 227. For other options, see Marshall D. Johnson, *The Purpose of the Biblical Genealogies* (Cambridge: Cambridge University Press, 1969), 207.

10. In this chiasm, days two and three and days five and six need to be combined for the chiastic relationships to be consistent. Otherwise the creation order of the fish and birds does not correspond to the order of sky and seas. Such a combination would be the kind of artful variation often found in Hebrew writ-

ing. It may be a pointer to encourage us to see something other than simply chronology in this text.

11. See Lee Irons with Meredith Kline, "The Framework View," 217–56.

12. Wenham, *Genesis 1–15*, 7.

13. This study is not the place to present the argument for a change in the Sabbath from the seventh to the first day. For a good presentation of that argument, see Joseph A. Pipa Jr., *The Lord's Day* (Fearn, Ross-shire, Great Britain: Christian Focus, 1997).

14. The NIV translation of Ex. 31:17, "on the seventh day he abstained from work and rested," is not satisfactory. It tames the strong statement in the Hebrew inappropriately.

15. For a fuller discussion of Ex. 31:17, see Irons and Kline, "The Framework View," *The Genesis Debate*, 249.

CHAPTER 3: THE MESSAGE OF GENESIS 1

1. This point is made in "The Report of the Committee to Study the Framework Hypothesis," presented to the Presbytery of Southern California of the Orthodox Presbyterian Church at its meeting on October 15–16, 1999, 8.

2. This point is made by E. J. Young, *Studies in Genesis 1* (Philadelphia: P&R, 1964), 104.

3. I am indebted to my colleague Bryan Estelle for drawing my attention to this element in the text.

4. The NIV translation is again weak on Gen. 2:4, rendering the word "day" as "when." The point made here about the meaning of "day" is not changed if the clause "in the day that the Lord God made earth and heaven" is attached to what follows it (as in the NIV) rather than to that which precedes it (as in the NASB).

5. Interestingly J. Ligon Duncan III and David W. Hall, "The Twenty-Four-Hour View," in *The Genesis Debate*, ed. David G. Hagopian (Mission Viejo, Calif.: Crux Press, 2001), 36, cite Gen. 5:1, "in the day God created man," apparently to argue that "day" means twenty-four hours and that man was created in one day. But they make no mention of Gen. 2:4, where day is used in exactly the same construction to refer to all of God's creative work.

6. This point is made effectively by Lee Irons with Meredith Kline, "The Framework View," in *The Genesis Debate,* ed. David G. Hagopian (Mission Viejo, Calif.: Crux Press, 2001), 282–83.

7. Duncan and Hall devote a great deal of time to this point in "The Twenty-Four-Hour View," *The Genesis Debate*.

8. One place where the days of creation are discussed in detail is in the apocryphal book 2 Esdras 6. But no such discussion is found in canonical Scripture. This section of 2 Esdras is quoted in full in appendix 2 of this study so that the reader can contrast the nonbiblical use of the days with the ways in which the Bible refers to the days.

9. I am indebted for this example to Irons with Kline, "The Framework View," *The Genesis Debate*, 243.

10. The purpose of appendix 1 of this study is to show that we have followed the interpretive methods of John Calvin in this study of Genesis 1.

APPENDIX 1: CALVIN ON CREATION FROM HIS COMMENTARY ON GENESIS 1

1. John Calvin, *Commentaries on the Four Last Books of Moses*, 4 vols. (Grand Rapids, Mich.: Baker, 1979), 1:78 (on Gen. 1:5).

2. Ibid., 92 (on Gen. 1:26).

3. Ibid., 77 (on Gen. 1:4); see also 91 (on Gen. 1:26).

4. Ibid., 100 (on Gen. 1:31).

5. Ibid., 85–86 (on Gen. 1:15).

6. Ibid., 96 (on Gen. 1:26).

7. Ibid., 105 (on Gen. 2:3).

8. Ibid., 80 (on Gen. 1:6).

9. Ibid., 86 (on Gen. 1:16).

10. Ibid.

11. Ibid., 88–89 (on Gen. 1:20).

12. Ibid., 105–6 (on Gen. 2:3).

13. Ibid., 103–4 (on Gen. 2:2).

14. Ibid., 104 (on Gen. 2:2).

15. Ibid., 76 (on Gen. 1:3).

16. Ibid., 82 (on Gen. 1:11).

17. Ibid.

APPENDIX 2: 2 ESDRAS 6:35–59

1. Cited from *The New Oxford Annotated Bible with the Apocrypha*, Revised Standard Version (New York: Oxford University Press, 1977).

APPENDIX 3: THE REFORMED CONFESSIONS ON CREATION

1. All Scripture quotations from the Second Helvetic Confession are from the King James Version of the Bible.

APPENDIX 4: "SIX DAYS" IN THE WESTMINSTER STANDARDS

1. Thomas Ridgeley, *Commentary on the Larger Catechism* (Edmonton, Alberta, Canada: Still Waters Revival Books, 1993), 1:331–32.

2. Thomas Boston, *Commentary on the Shorter Catechism* (Edmonton, Alberta, Canada: Still Waters Revival Books, 1993), 1:173.

3. Ashbel Green, *Lectures on the Shorter Catechism of the Presbyterian Church in the United States of America Addressed to Youth* (Philadelphia: Presbyterian Board of Publication and Sabbath-School Work, 1841), 1:195, 198.

4. Robert Shaw, *The Reformed Faith: An Exposition of The Westminster Confession of Faith* (Inverness, Scotland: Christian Focus, 1974), 61, 62.

5. A. A. Hodge, *The Confession of Faith* (London: The Banner of Truth Trust, 1958), 82–83.

6. John Macpherson, *The Westminster Confession of Faith* (Edinburgh: T & T Clark, 1977), 52–53.

7. James Harper, *An Exposition in the Form of Question and Answer of the Westminster Assembly's Shorter Catechism* (Pittsburgh: United Presbyterian Board of Publication, 1905), 67–68.

8. G. I. Williamson, *The Westminster Confession of Faith for Study Classes* (Philadelphia: P&R, 1964), 42–43.

9. Gordon H. Clark, *What Do Presbyterians Believe?* (Phillipsburg, N.J.: P&R, 1979), 58–59.

10. David W. Hall, "What Was the View of the Westminster Assembly Divines on Creation Days?" in *Did God Create in Six Days?* ed. Joseph A. Pipa Jr. and David W. Hall (Taylors, S.C.: Southern Presbyterian Press, 1999), 41.

11. William S. Barker, "The Westminster Assembly on the Days of Creation: A Reply to David W. Hall," *The Westminster Theological Journal* 62 (2000), 114–15.

W. Robert Godfrey (Ph.D., Stanford University) is professor of church history and president of Westminster Theological Seminary in California. He is a minister of the United Reformed Churches. He is the author of *Reformation Sketches: Insights into Luther, Calvin, and the Confessions,* coeditor of *Theonomy: A Reformed Critique,* and contributor to *John Calvin: His Influence in the Western World.* Godfrey has also written numerous articles. He has been a speaker at many conferences, including the Lausanne Committee for World Evangelization, the Philadelphia Conference on Reformed Theology, and Ligonier Ministries.